THE COMPLETE INSTANT POT MEAL PREP COOKBOOK

Betty Brown

Warning-Disclaimer

The purpose of this book is to educate and entertain. The author or publisher does not guarantee that anyone following the techniques, suggestions, tips, ideas, or strategies will become successful. The author and publisher shall have neither liability or responsibility to anyone with respect to any loss or damage caused, or alleged to be caused, directly or indirectly by the information contained in this book.

CONTENTS

INTRODUCTION

Do you want to make the leap from good to great in your kitchen? Are you dreaming of making complete meals before you can say Jack Robinson? An Instant Pot and meal prep come to fulfill your needs!

The Instant Pot is a modern-day invention that performs various cooking tasks such as steaming, sautéing, boiling, slow cooking, baking, and so forth. The Instant Pot utilizes a super-heated steam and high pressure to cook the best one-pot meals ever. This revolutionary kitchen gadget can significantly cut cooking time, save electricity, and help you eat healthier.

If you want to make well-balanced and delicious meals for you and your family, but you are confused by all the information out there, this recipe collection can transform your life forever.

This cookbook may help you make your cooking routine more efficient and eat healthier. It contains 105 meal prep ideas to keep your belly full, your family happy, and your finances on track.

Who doesn't savor a peaceful family weekend? However, getting family meals on the table is a daily challenge! You can feel stressed about coking during your busy week, trying to make something healthy and nutritious when you do not have time to cook. Therefore, your first instinct is to order takeout or make a quick, unhealthy meal in your microwave. On the other hand, you can take some time on the weekend to prepare food in advance for the week. Thanks to the Instant Pot, eating well has been a part of daily lives for many families worldwide. Come and join us! Welcome to the sophisticated casseroles, homey soups, as well as decadent appetizers and the best desserts around! Welcome to the wonderful world of meal prepping and pressure cooking!

GETTING STARTED: HOW TO USE THE INSTANT POT

The Instant Pot is a unique piece of cooking equipment designed to cook food under pressure. Pressure cooking is all about texture and flavors, and about getting amazing results! What can be cooked with the Instant Pot?

From grab-and-go breakfast, an amazing family lunch, and romantic dinner to fast snacks and desserts, you can cook almost all your meals in the Instant Pot. Simply put, you can cook a delicious family meal in less than 15 or 30 minutes. The versatility of the Instant Pot is so inspiring!

Favorite family dishes such as risotto, pasta, chili or stew can be prepared in 30 to 40 minutes, start to finish. Of course, you can bake a cake with the Instant Pot or whip up a fantastic pudding. Keto and paleo dieters, vegans and nutritionists, we all love the Instant Pot for its ability to cook complete meals in no time. For instance, dry beans can be cooked in 30 minutes in the Instant Pot.

The Instant Pot has the delay timer and a set of pre-set smart cooking programs. There are fifteen fully automated cooking programs, which may be available depending on the model of your Instant Pot: Steam, Soup/Broth, Meat/Stew, Pressure Cook/ Manual, Bean/Chili, Multigrain, Porridge, Yogurt, Rice, Slow Cook, Sauté, Egg, Cake, Sterilize, and Keep Warm. It sounds like a dream, but there are some rules to keep in mind before starting this adventure. What we've learned from user's suggestions, tips, and hints?

> You need to understand the particulars of your model so read the manufacturer's manual thoroughly.

> When it comes to the rice and grains, pay attention to a water to grain ratio. It's not the same as it is for the conventional cooking methods.

> For vegetables, use the "Steam" setting; feel free to cook them straight from the freezer.

> Drizzle a tablespoon or two of oil over beans and legumes to keep them from foaming up as they cook.

> Remember – liquid is the key. The amount of liquid depends on food in your inner pot and the cooking time. Generally, use a minimum of 1 cup liquid, such as water, broth or alcohol (avoid high-alcohol liquors because they can create vapor). It's better to be safe than sorry; so if you end up with too much cooking juices, you can thicken them on the "Sauté" function. However, do

not use pureed vegetables such as tomato puree as the only cooking liquid because they do not have enough water and they can easily burn in your Instant Pot.

➤ Always keep track of progress, especially if you are at the very beginning, by using the display on the front of your cooker.

TOP FIVE BENEFITS OF THE INSTANT POT

There are many good reasons to love an Instant Pot, so treat this list as just the beginning. Once you get the hang of it, your list will expand.

1) An easy and genius way to eat healthier.

Most of us are trying to cook healthier and better, right? Undoubtedly, one of the key elements to a good, happy and healthy life is to eat a well-balanced diet on a regular basis. Cooking at home can help you stay healthy, lose weight, and prevent some serious diseases. Many studies found that people who eat homemade meals consume far fewer calories than those who often eat out.

One of the most important advantages of electric pressure cookers is their ability to preserve nutrients of food. Why is that so important to us?

Researchers have announced that cooking in a pressure cooker tends to keep a nutritive value of foods better than conventional cooking methods. The liquids come to a boil in a sealed space, raising the pressure inside the inner pot; that super-heated steam helps your food to retain its natural vitamins and minerals. Then, it is obvious that a shorter cooking time also helps preserve the nutrients. The last but not least, pressure cooking requires less oil, which makes it an exceptionally healthy cooking technique.

2) A wide variety of delicious homemade meals.

We know the facts: cooking at home is inexpensive and fun, it is better for your health and the environment!

With your Instant Pot, the flavor and aroma become excellent and vibrant, requiring just a little bit of add-ins. You can use only natural flavorings and have amazing results!

Juicy and tender meat, succulent poultry, and ooey gooey desserts are what pressure cooking is all about. In addition to being an excellent cooking method for tough cuts of meat, the Instant Pot allows you to cook delicate seafood and vegetable, which require more carefulness and precise cooking times. In addition, vegetables still have their crunch and bright colors. You can easily cook even the most sophisticated desserts! You will get great results, time and time again. When's the last time you saw traditional cooking methods do that?

3) Redefine set-it and forget-it meals.

The Instant Pot is a seven-in-one multi-cooker. We can sauté vegetables, caramelize onions, brown meat, build the sauce, and create the best breakfasts without a second pan. You don't have to clean up another cookware so you will spend less time in the kitchen. There is no greater satisfaction than throwing our favorite food into an Instant Pot, setting it, and going about your day!

4) The Instant Pot really does save time in the kitchen.

The Instant Pot can cook foods up to five times faster than conventional cooking methods! Butch cooking is another advantage of the Instant Pot, which can save you a lot of time. It is like having an extra burner or oven in your kitchen. In addition, your hands are free for other things!

5) Go green and declutter your kitchen!

Eco-friendly cooking is healthier for both, people and the environment. The Instant Pot is an eco-friendly electric device because it uses less electricity and it cooks inexpensive foods to perfection.

The Instant Pot is a multi-cooker so you will not need too much cookware in the future. This is a great way to free up your space and simplify your life.

MASTER THE ART OF MEAL PREP

The weekends are a wonderful opportunity to spend more time with our family and friends, enjoy favorite food, and spread some extra cheer. However, these days can also be a source of stress, especially if you need to cook for a big family.

Luckily, with the Instant Pot and the recipes in this cookbook, you can take a "shortcut" in preparing the best meals ever! The best part, though? You can fulfill all your nutritional needs and have the extra time for your loved ones. It's a step-by-step process so start slowly, set realistic kitchen goals and enjoy the process. You can do that by simply cooking your favorite meal and freeze leftovers for later. Next, you can make a plan for the week and cook two meals (more than you really need) in advance: then, you can refrigerate or freeze portions for busy weeknights.

You can cook multiple meals at the same time and save tons of time in the kitchen. Thanks to the Instant Pot, you can cook enough food for a week or month. Here are some great tips that may come in handy.

Seven Chef-Approved Tips for Faster Meal Prep

1) Invest in good storage containers.

Make sure to purchase good storage containers because they can keep the food fresh for days in the refrigerator and protected from freezer burn in your freezer. Quality glass containers are worth their investment but BPA-free plastic containers are also fine.

Opt for meal-prep friendly containers that allow you to portion-size your meals so you can eat directly from them. Good containers will allow you to have fall-back meals on hand when you don't feel like cooking. It could be as simple as a spinach omelet, chicken soup or nacho dip. If you have a small freezer, storage bags are better than plastic containers.

2) Declutter your kitchen.

Empty your dishwasher, take out the trash, and clean your kitchen so you will be able to work efficiently. This is a free and easy way to improve your home cooking and meal prep! Cleanup becomes a breeze with meal prepping as well. Less mess, less stress!

3) Plan a weekly menu.

The old adage is true: Preparation is half the battle! In fact, it requires a little pre-planning to ensure you're making healthy choices during your busy week. By making multiple portions of staple foods in advance, you can easily create a meal plan and get dinner on the table every night. This is a great way to lose weight as well. Meal prepping and batch cooking are great ways to balance your diet; they lower the chances to order take outs or buy some foods in the store. No boxes and cans anymore!

4) Try batch cooking.

Batch cooking and preparing multiple servings all at once are the key elements for successful dieting! It reduces time, minimizes food waste, saves your budget, and keeps you on track. Simply buy in bulk and choose cheap cuts of meat because the Instant pot can turn them into great-tasting meals. What about multi-tasking in the kitchen?

For instance, you can cook a few batches of rice or bulgur and place it in your refrigerator. Then, you can divide them into containers and place in the freezer. When ready to reheat, you have your own homemade 5-minute meals!

Further, you can create 2 to 3 sauces on Sunday and mix them with meats and vegetables during the week. Prepare a horseradish mayo, tzatziki, or marinara and use them to create a different meal every day.

5) Get creative in the kitchen.

Did you know that leftovers can make flavorful salads? Prepare large cuts of meats or tofu and use them for a family lunch; then, place in the refrigerator and allow them to cool completely; on an actual day, use cold meat to make a salad for dinner.

Use leftover bacon, cheese and stale bread to make a delicious casserole; then, freeze portions for the next week.

Gather all the leftover vegetables and nuts from your holiday recipes, and add them to cooked couscous along with seasonings; then, freeze the portions. Serve with grilled fish or pork chops throughout the week.

6) Make things ahead of time.

If you have your staple ingredients at your fingertips, it could be a great time-saving solution. You can simply pre-freeze your favorite ingredients. Chop up your fruits or vegetables and put them into a freezer bag. Throw your supplies into a blender in the morning and you will have an easy and healthy breakfast. You can also make smoothie ice cubes by blending leftover fruit, nuts and vegetables and pouring the content into ice cube molds. Add these cubes to your smoothie bowl, juice or fruit salad.

On the other hand, making a soup or vegan chili become much faster when your vegetables are chopped in advance. In addition, it is cheaper than buying pre-cut vegetables at the store.

7) Take advantage of your Instant Pot.

The Instant Pot is a multi-cooker that cooks super convenient meals easily and quickly. Use your Instant Pot to make extra-large lasagna or a giant pot of stew. The Instant Pot perfectly cooks big batches of proteins, vegetables, whole grains, and beans. In addition, these foods reheat well and tend to get better as leftovers! A beef stew often tastes better the next day, right?

Meal prepping and cooking homemade meals in the Instant Pot allow you to control your eating on a daily basis.

A WORD ABOUT OUR RECIPE COLLECTION

This recipe collection offers 105 tasty cooking solutions so you will find a lot of inspiration and creative ideas to make your meal prepping fun and super-easy.

At the start of each recipe, we list the following: the number of servings, cooking time, and nutritional information. Please note that the cooking time is for how long the instant Pot stays at pressure; it does not count the time it takes it to get to the pressure (it is between 5 and 20 minutes). This recipe collection follows the global culinary trends, it will give you the guidelines to get the most out of the Instant Pot and meal prepping.

Cooking is a lifelong adventure so be prepared to learn by trial and error. Read each recipe from start to finish before you grab your Instant Pot. With this recipe collection as your guide, successful meal prep is guaranteed. Before you know it, you will be making healthy foods, planning your meals, and creating the best family moments ever!

The Complete Instant Pot Meal Prep Cookbook

BREAKFAST

1. CAULIFLOWER AND CHEESE FRITTATA

4 Servings

Ready in about
30 minutes

PER SERVING:
489 Calories; 41.2g Fat;
10.2g Carbs; 21g Protein;
4.6g Sugars

Two types of cheese, cauliflower and eggs are all cooked together in this amazingly delicious frittata for a savory breakfast.

Ingredients

- 1 cup cream cheese, room temperature
- 5 eggs, beaten
- 2 tablespoons olive oil
- 1/2 cup scallions, chopped
- 1 teaspoon garlic, minced

- Sea salt and ground black pepper, to your liking
- 1/2 teaspoon cayenne pepper
- 1/4 teaspoon dried dill weed
- 1 cup Swiss cheese, shredded
- 1 head cauliflower, cut into florets

Directions

1. Add 1 cup of water and the metal trivet to your Instant Pot Spritz a baking pan with a nonstick cooking spray.

2. Thoroughly combine cream cheese with eggs and olive oil. Now, add scallions, garlic, salt, black pepper, cayenne pepper, and dill; mix to combine well.

3. After that, stir in Swiss cheese and cauliflower. Mix to combine and spoon the mixture into the prepared baking pan.

4. Lower the baking pan onto the trivet and secure the lid. Choose "Manual" function, High pressure and 10 minutes.

5. Once cooking is complete, use a natural release for 15 minutes; remove the lid carefully. Let cool completely.

Storing

1. Cut the frittata into four wedges. Place each of them in an airtight container; place in the refrigerator for up 3 to 4 days.

2. To freeze, place in separate Ziploc bags and freeze up to 3 months. To defrost, place in your microwave for a few minutes.

2. CHOCOLATE BANANA OATMEAL

4 Servings

Ready in about
15 minutes

PER SERVING:
193 Calories; 6.6g Fat;
37.2g Carbs; 10.3g
Protein; 10.8g Sugars

A chocolate dessert for breakfast?! Yes, please! Top your oatmeal with banana and start your day off right!

Ingredients

- 1 ½ cups steel-cut oats
- 2 cups chocolate milk
- 2 cups water
- 1/3 cup dark chocolate chips
- 1/2 teaspoon ground cinnamon

- 1/8 teaspoon salt
- 1/4 teaspoon crystallized ginger
- 1/8 teaspoon grated nutmeg
- 1 large banana, thinly sliced

Directions

1. Throw all of the above ingredients, except banana, in your Instant Pot.

2. Secure the lid. Choose the "Manual" mode and cook for 5 minutes under High pressure. Once cooking is complete, use a natural pressure release; carefully remove the lid.

3. Taste and adjust the sweetness. Top with sliced banana. Let cool completely.

Storing

1. Spoon the oatmeal into four airtight containers; keep in your refrigerator for up to 4 to 6 days.

2. For freezing, place the oatmeal in airtight containers or heavy-duty freezer bags. It will maintain the best quality for about 6 months. Defrost in the refrigerator. Enjoy!

3. EASY MONKEY BREAD

8 Servings

Ready in about
25 minutes

PER SERVING:
283 Calories; 9.1g Fat;
49.2g Carbs; 2.5g Protein;
28.9g Sugars

A finger-licking-good sweet bread that is ready in just about 25 minutes! It's hard to believe that a store-bought biscuit dough can make such a flavorful meal.

Ingredients

- 1 (12-ounce) package biscuit dough, cut in quarters
- 2/3 cup white sugar
- 1 teaspoon apple pie spice
- 1/4 cup coconut oil
- 1/3 cup brown sugar
- A pinch of coarse salt

Directions

1. Prepare your Instant Pot by adding 1 cup of water and a metal trivet to its bottom.

2. Coat biscuit dough with white sugar evenly. Arrange the biscuit pieces in a fluted tube pan that is previously greased with a nonstick cooking spray.

3. In a mixing bowl, thoroughly combine apple pie spice, coconut oil, brown sugar, and salt; microwave for 40 to 50 seconds or until butter is melted.

4. Spread this butter sauce over the biscuit pieces. Place the fluted tube pan onto the trivet; cover the top with a foil.

5. Secure the lid. Choose the "Manual" mode and cook for 22 minutes under High pressure. Once cooking is complete, use a natural pressure release; carefully remove the lid. Let cool completely.

Storing

1. Place your bread in a breadbox or wrap in foil; store for about 2 to 3 days at normal room temperature.

2. Place in a storage bag and transfer to your refrigerator; it will last for 2 to 3 days before getting stale.

3. For freezing, slice your bread and wrap tightly with foil or plastic freezer wrap. It will maintain the best quality for about 3 months.

4. CREAMY SCRAMBLED EGGS WITH RICOTTA

4 Servings

Ready in about
10 minutes

PER SERVING:
205 Calories; 16.1g Fat;
2.7g Carbs; 12.1g Protein;
0.9g Sugars

It's hard to beat scrambled eggs for a fast and easy nutrition-packed breakfast. We added fresh ricotta cheese to make it even better.

Ingredients

- 2 tablespoons butter, at room temperature
- 6 whole eggs
- Sat and ground black pepper, to taste

- 1/2 teaspoon paprika
- 1/2 cup ricotta cheese, crumbled
- 2 tablespoons fresh parsley leaves, roughly chopped

Directions

1. Press the "Sauté" button to preheat the Instant Pot. Melt the butter and add beaten eggs.

2. Add the salt, black pepper and paprika; stir to combine well. Scramble the eggs in the Instant Pot using a wide spatula.

3. Secure the lid. Choose the "Manual" mode and cook for 5 minutes under High pressure. Once cooking is complete, use a quick pressure release; carefully remove the lid; top with fresh chopped parsley.

4. Let cool completely.

Storing

1. Divide scrambled eggs between four airtight containers or Ziploc bags. Refrigerate for up to 3 days.

2. For freezing, place scrambled eggs in four Ziploc bags and freeze up to 3 months. Defrost in the microwave for a few minutes.

5. Breakfast Muffins with Bacon

6 Servings

Ready in about
15 minutes

PER SERVING:
305 Calories; 26.1g Fat;
8.9g Carbs; 10.2g Protein;
5.8g Sugars

Insured by Italian flavors, you can come out with these great crustless muffins. It's easy to customize this recipe!

Ingredients

- 6 bacon slices
- 3/4 cup tomato paste
- 1 cup cream cheese

- 1/2 cup cheddar cheese, grated
- 1 tablespoon Italian seasoning
- 8 olives, pitted and sliced

Directions

1. Add 1 cup of water and a trivet to the bottom of your Instant Pot.

2. Add 1 slice of bacon to each silicone mold. Divide the remaining ingredients among silicone molds.

3. Lower the silicone molds onto the trivet.

4. Secure the lid. Choose "Manual" mode and High pressure; cook for 8 minutes. Once cooking is complete, use a quick pressure release; carefully remove the lid. Let cool completely.

Storing

1. Place your muffins in the airtight containers or Ziploc bags; keep in the refrigerator for a week.

2. For freezing, divide your muffins among three Ziploc bags and freeze up to 3 months. Defrost in your microwave for a couple of minutes. Bon appétit!

6. SUMMER BREAD WITH YOGURT

8 Servings

Ready in about
4 hours 30 minutes

PER SERVING:
205 Calories; 0.6g Fat;
40.9g Carbs; 7.7g Protein;
1.1g Sugars

This bread is a perfect accompaniment to any Greek meal. Serve with feta cheese, Kalamata olives, or grilled eggplant. On the next day, you can reheat this bread approximately 10 minutes at 350 degrees F in the preheated oven.

Ingredients

- 3 1/3 cups all-purpose flour
- 1 teaspoon kosher salt
- 1 teaspoon white sugar
- 1 teaspoon instant yeast
- 1 cup water
- 1 cup Greek-style yogurt
- 1 teaspoon dried oregano

Directions

1. Thoroughly combine the flour, salt, sugar, and yeast.

2. Pour in the water and yogurt; add dried oregano; knead the mixture by hand until a ball of dough is formed.

3. Line the inside of the Instant Pot with a piece of parchment paper; place the dough in your Instant Pot.

4. Secure the lid. Choose the "Yogurt" mode and High pressure; cook for 4 hours. Once cooking is complete, use a natural pressure release; carefully remove the lid.

5. Bake your bread in the preheated oven at 450 degrees F for 25 minutes. Transfer to a rack and allow it to cool completely.

Storing

1. Place your bread in a breadbox or wrap in foil; store for about 2 to 3 days at normal room temperature.

2. Place in a storage bag and transfer to your refrigerator; it will last for 2 to 3 days before getting stale.

3. For freezing, wrap the loaf with clear plastic bread bags. Freeze up to 3 months. To thaw the frozen bread, let it come to room temperature.

4. Just before serving, place your bread in an oven heated to 400 degrees F for about 4 minutes.

7. Rich Casserole Italiano

5 Servings

Ready in about
30 minutes

PER SERVING:
549 Calories; 39.9g
Fat; 25.8g Carbs; 23.4g
Protein; 3.5g Sugars

Keep this recipe in your back pocket! For an extra indulgence, serve with a slice of a homemade crusty bread.

Ingredients

- 1 tablespoon olive oil
- 4 ounces Italian salami, chopped
- 1 red bell pepper, seeded and chopped
- 1 green bell pepper, seeded and chopped
- 1 Peperoncino, seeded and chopped
- 2 ½ cups hash browns, frozen
- 5 eggs
- 1/3 cup milk
- 3/4 cup cream cheese, at room temperature
- Sea salt and ground black pepper, to taste
- 1/2 teaspoon dried basil
- 1/2 teaspoon dried oregano
- 1/2 teaspoon paprika

Directions

1. Press the "Sauté" button to preheat the Instant Pot. Now, heat the oil until sizzling. Cook salami for 2 minutes or until crispy.

2. Add peppers and hash browns; stir and continue to cook for a further 3 minutes.

3. Spritz the bottom and sides of a casserole dish with a nonstick cooking spray. Scrape the hash brown mixture into the dish.

4. In a mixing bowl, thoroughly combine the eggs, milk, cheese, salt, black pepper, basil, oregano, and paprika. Pour the mixture into the casserole dish.

5. Add 1 ½ cups of water and a metal rack to the Instant Pot. Lower the casserole dish onto the rack.

6. Secure the lid. Choose the "Meat/Stew" mode and cook for 20 minutes under High pressure. Once cooking is complete, use a quick pressure release; carefully remove the lid. Let cool completely.

Storing

1. Slice the casserole into five pieces. Divide the pieces between airtight containers; it will last for 3 to 4 days in the refrigerator.

2. For freezing, place each portion in a separate heavy-duty freezer bag. Freeze up to 2 to 3 months. Defrost in the microwave or refrigerator. Bon appétit!

8. Vegan Chocolate Oatmeal

4 Servings

Ready in about
15 minutes

PER SERVING:
247 Calories; 11.6g
Fat; 39.8g Carbs; 10.9g
Protein; 14.3g Sugars

Here's a nutritious and delicious breakfast on the fly! Garnish with some extra dried fruits, nuts or seeds, if desired.

Ingredients

- 1 ½ cups rolled oats
- 2 cups water
- 2 cups almond milk
- 1 teaspoon carob powder
- 3 teaspoons cocoa powder

- 1/2 teaspoon cinnamon, ground
- 1/4 teaspoon star anise, ground
- 1/2 teaspoon pure vanilla extract
- 1/2 cup dark chocolate chips

Directions

1. Simply throw all of the above ingredients, except for chocolate chips, into your Instant Pot; stir to combine well.

2. Secure the lid. Choose the "Manual" mode. Cook for 10 minutes at High pressure. Once cooking is complete, use a natural release; carefully remove the lid.

3. Top with dark chocolate chips. Let cool completely.

Storing

1. Spoon the oatmeal into four airtight containers; keep in your refrigerator for up to 4 to 6 days.

2. For freezing, place the oatmeal in airtight containers or heavy-duty freezer bags. It will maintain the best quality for about 6 months. Defrost in the refrigerator. Enjoy!

9. Vegetable Frittata with Canadian Bacon

4 Servings

Ready in about
25 minutes

PER SERVING:
429 Calories; 30.5g
Fat; 11.3g Carbs; 28.1g
Protein; 5.6g Sugars

A no-fuss homemade meal for the whole family! Transform a standard frittata into a real masterpiece using your Instant Pot.

Ingredients

- 6 ounces Canadian bacon, chopped
- 2 bell peppers, chopped
- 1 red chili pepper, seeded and chopped
- 1 carrot, trimmed and chopped
- 1 yellow onion, peeled and chopped
- 1/2 cup Kalamata olives, pitted and sliced
- 5 eggs

- 1/2 cup double cream
- Sea salt and ground pepper, to taste
- 1/2 teaspoon cayenne pepper
- 1 teaspoon dried parsley flakes
- 1/2 teaspoon dried oregano
- 1 1/3 cup Colby cheese, grated

Directions

1. Prepare your Instant Pot by adding 1 ½ cups of water and a metal rack to its bottom.

2. Then, add bacon and vegetables to a lightly greased baking pan.

3. In a mixing bowl, whisk the eggs with double cream, salt, black pepper, cayenne pepper, parsley, and oregano.

4. Pour the egg/cheese mixture over your vegetables in the Instant Pot. Top with grated cheese.

5. Secure the lid. Choose the "Manual" mode and cook for 21 minutes under High pressure. Once cooking is complete, use a natural pressure release; carefully remove the lid. Let cool completely.

Storing

1. Cut the frittata into four wedges. Place each of them in an airtight container; place in the refrigerator for up 3 to 4 days.

2. To freeze, place in separate Ziploc bags and freeze up to 3 months. To defrost, place in your microwave for a few minutes.

10. CHRISTMAS MORNING CORNBREAD

8 Servings

Ready in about
35 minutes

PER SERVING:
191 Calories; 5.9g Fat;
29.2g Carbs; 5.1g Protein;
5.5g Sugars

This sweet cornbread is the perfect festive food! Loaded with eggs, canned corn and golden syrup, it will give you more than you could expect from a cornbread recipe.

Ingredients

- 1/2 cup cornmeal
- 2/3 cup all-purpose flour
- 2 teaspoons baking powder
- 1/2 teaspoon salt
- 2 tablespoons sugar

- 3 teaspoons margarine, melted
- 1/4 cup heavy cream
- 2 eggs, beaten
- 2 tablespoons golden syrup
- 1/2 cup canned corn

Directions

1. Combine dry ingredients in a bowl. In another bowl, thoroughly combine wet ingredients. Mix the dry mixture with wet mixture.

2. Spritz a round baking pan with a nonstick cooking spray. Scrape the batter into the prepared pan. Cover with aluminum foil, making a foil sling.

3. Add 1 cup of water and a metal trivet to the Instant Pot.

4. Secure the lid. Choose the "Multigrain" mode and High pressure; cook for 20 minutes. Once cooking is complete, use a quick pressure release; carefully remove the lid.

5. Transfer to a wire rack to sit for 5 to 10 minutes.

Storing

1. Place your cornbread in a breadbox or wrap in foil; store for about 1 to 2 days at room temperature.

2. Place in a storage bag and transfer to your refrigerator; it will last for 1 week before getting stale.

3. For freezing, wrap the loaf with clear plastic bread bags. Freeze up to 2 to 3 months. To thaw the frozen cornbread, let it come to room temperature.

4. Just before serving, place your cornbread in an oven heated to 400 degrees F for about 4 minutes.

11. Two-Cheese Polenta

4 Servings

Ready in about
15 minutes

PER SERVING:
502 Calories; 22.1g
Fat; 54.2g Carbs; 20.3g
Protein; 4.6g Sugars

This polenta is easy to make and tastes so good. A great idea for a family breakfast!
This is the perfect opportunity to break that take out habit!

Ingredients

- 6 cups roasted vegetable broth
- 1/2 stick butter, softened
- 1 ½ cups cornmeal
- Sea salt and ground black pepper, to taste
- 1 cup Cheddar cheese, shredded
- 1/2 cup Ricotta cheese, at room temperature

Directions

1. Press the "Sauté" button to preheat the Instant Pot. Then, add the broth and butter; bring to a boil. Slowly and gradually, whisk in the cornmeal. Season with the salt and pepper.

2. Secure the lid. Choose the "Manual" mode and High pressure; cook for 8 minutes. Once cooking is complete, use a natural pressure release; carefully remove the lid.

3. Top with cheese. Let cool completely.

Storing

1. Spoon the polenta into four airtight containers; keep in your refrigerator for up to 4 days.

2. For freezing, scrape the polenta into a food storage container and use frozen polenta within a few weeks for best results. Defrost in the refrigerator. Enjoy!

12. HUMMUS WITH RICOTTA AND HERBS

10 Servings

Ready in about
45 minutes

PER SERVING:
153 Calories; 5.7g Fat;
19.8g Carbs; 6.7g Protein;
3.3g Sugars

This delicious dip can be made one week ahead. To make it last longer, drizzle a tablespoon of two of olive oil over the top and place your hummus in the refrigerator.

Ingredients

- 1 ½ cups dried garbanzo beans, soaked overnight
- 4 cups water
- 1/4 cup extra-virgin olive oil
- 2 tablespoons light tahini
- 2 tablespoons fresh lemon juice
- 1 teaspoon garlic, minced
- 1 teaspoon onion powder

- 1/2 teaspoon dried dill weed
- 1/2 teaspoon dried oregano
- 1/2 teaspoon cumin powder
- 1 teaspoon spicy brown mustard
- 1 teaspoon kosher salt
- 1/3 cup ricotta cheese
- 1/2 teaspoon red chili pepper

Directions

1. Add soaked garbanzo beans with 4 cups of water to your Instant Pot.

2. Secure the lid and choose the "Bean/Chili" function; cook for 40 minutes at High pressure. Once cooking is complete, use a natural release; carefully remove the lid.

3. Drain garbanzo beans, reserving cooking liquid. Transfer chickpeas to your food processor. Add olive oil, tahini, lemon juice, garlic, onion powder, dill weed, oregano, cumin powder, mustard, and salt.

4. Add ricotta cheese and about 1 cup of cooking liquid; process until everything is creamy and smooth. Sprinkle red chili pepper over the top. Let cool completely.

Storing

1. Spoon your hummus into airtight containers; keep in your refrigerator for up to 4 to 7 days.

2. For freezing, place your hummus in airtight containers or heavy-duty freezer bags. It will maintain the best quality for about 3 to 4 months. Defrost in the refrigerator. Enjoy!

13. AROMATIC COCONUT BREAD PUDDING

8 Servings

Ready in about
25 minutes

PER SERVING:
333 Calories; 7.2g Fat;
53.7g Carbs; 13.4g
Protein; 16.5g Sugars

This breakfast will bring the tropical flavors into your kitchen!
Serve in individual bowls, drizzled with some extra honey.

Ingredients

- Nonstick cooking spray
- 3 eggs, beaten
- 3/4 cup almond milk
- 1/4 cup honey
- 1 teaspoon pure vanilla extract
- 1/2 teaspoon pure coconut extract
- 1/2 teaspoon ground cinnamon
- 1/4 teaspoon grated nutmeg

- 1/2 teaspoon ground cardamom
- 1 tablespoon finely grated orange zest
- A pinch of salt
- 1 loaf day-old challah bread, cubed into 1-inch pieces
- 1/2 cup sweetened shredded coconut
- 4 tablespoons crushed pineapple, drained

Directions

1. Spritz the sides and bottom of a baking pan with a nonstick cooking spray.

2. In a mixing bowl, whisk eggs with almond milk, honey, vanilla, coconut extract, cinnamon, cardamom, orange zest, and salt.

3. Stir in bread pieces along with shredded coconut and crushed pineapple; press down into pan slightly.

4. Cover the baking pan with a sheet of foil and make a foil sling. Add 1 cup of water and the metal trivet to the Instant Pot.

5. Lower the baking pan onto the trivet. Secure the lid. Choose the "Manual" mode, High pressure, and 20 minutes. Once cooking is complete, use a quick release; carefully remove the lid.

6. Let cool completely.

Storing

1. Spoon bread pudding into four airtight containers; keep in your refrigerator for up to 5 to 6 days.

2. For freezing, place bread pudding in airtight containers or heavy-duty freezer bags. It will maintain the best quality for about 2 to 3 months. Defrost in your refrigerator. Bon appétit!

14. BANANA BREAD WITH PECANS

8 Servings

Ready in about
15 minutes

PER SERVING:
485 Calories; 13.3g Fat;
89.3g Carbs; 6.3g Protein;
42.7g Sugars

You can always swap out pecans for almonds and walnuts, or toss in chocolate chips. Start by making the recipe as written; the next time you can adjust it according to your taste.

Ingredients

- 2 ½ cups cake flour
- 1 teaspoon baking soda
- 1/2 teaspoon baking powder
- 1/8 teaspoon kosher salt
- 1/4 teaspoon grated nutmeg
- 1/2 teaspoon ground cinnamon
- 1 pound ripe bananas, mashed
- 1 tablespoon fresh lemon juice

- 1 stick butter, at room temperature
- 1 cup sugar
- 1/2 cup maple syrup
- 2 eggs plus 1 egg yolk, beaten
- 1/2 teaspoon vanilla paste
- 1 teaspoon rum extract
- 1 1/3 cups soy milk
- 2 tablespoons pecans, ground

Directions

1. Add water and a metal trivet to the Instant Pot. Spritz a bread loaf pan with a nonstick cooking spray.

2. In a mixing bowl, thoroughly combine cake flour, baking soda, baking powder, salt, nutmeg, and cinnamon.

3. In another mixing bowl, mix mashed bananas with fresh lemon juice; reserve.

4. Now, cream the butter with sugar and maple syrup using an electric mixer. Fold in the eggs and mix again until smooth and uniform.

5. Stir in vanilla, rum extract, soy milk, and ground pecans.

6. Then, stir in the dry flour mixture, and combine well. Afterwards, stir in the banana/lemon mixture and mix again.

7. Scrape the batter into the prepared pan. Lower the pan onto the trivet and secure the lid.

8. Choose the "Manual" mode; bake for 1 hour at High pressure. Once cooking is complete, use a natural release for 15 minutes; carefully remove the lid.

9. Transfer the pan to a wire rack to cool before storing.

Storing

1. Place banana bread in a breadbox or wrap in foil; store for about 1 to 2 days at room temperature.

2. Place banana bread in a storage bag and transfer to your refrigerator; it will last for 1 week before getting stale.

3. For freezing, wrap the loaf with clear plastic bread bags. Freeze up to 2 to 3 months. To thaw the frozen banana bread, let it come to room temperature. Bon appétit!

15. Sweet Porridge with Seeds

4 Servings

Ready in about
15 minutes

PER SERVING:
379 Calories; 23.7g Fat;
50.6g Carbs; 9.4g Protein;
23.6g Sugars

Rich and satisfying, this pressure cooked porridge is dairy free, vegan, and extremely healthy, which makes it a great idea for a family breakfast.

Ingredients

- 1 ½ cups rolled oats
- 1 ½ cups coconut milk
- 2 cups water
- 1/2 teaspoon pure vanilla extract
- 1/2 teaspoon ground cinnamon
- 1/4 teaspoon grated nutmeg

- 1/8 teaspoon kosher salt
- 1/3 cup agave nectar
- 1 tablespoon flaxseeds
- 1 tablespoon sunflower seeds
- 1 tablespoon pumpkin seeds

Directions

1. Add all of the above ingredients to your Instant Pot.

2. Secure the lid. Choose the "Manual" mode. Cook for 10 minutes at High pressure. Once cooking is complete, use a natural release; carefully remove the lid.

3. Let cool completely.

Storing

1. Spoon your porridge into four airtight containers; keep in your refrigerator for up to 4 to 6 days.

2. For freezing, place your porridge in airtight containers or heavy-duty freezer bags. It will maintain the best quality for about 6 months. Defrost in the refrigerator. Bon appétit!

16. Brioche French Toast with Blackberries

6 Servings

Ready in about
25 minutes

PER SERVING:
435 Calories; 28.4g
Fat; 35.6g Carbs; 12.2g
Protein; 30.9g Sugars

Need more breakfast ideas? This breakfast staple has all the flavors of traditional French toast with none of the hassle.

Ingredients

- 1 loaf Brioche bread, cubed
- 3/4 cup fresh blackberries
- 10 ounces Neufchâtel cheese, at room temperature
- 1/2 cup honey
- 3 eggs, beaten
- 1/2 teaspoon ground cinnamon
- 1/4 teaspoon grated nutmeg
- 1/2 cup milk
- 1/2 cup applesauce
- 1 stick butter, cold

Directions

1. Start by adding 1 cup of water and a metal rack to the bottom of your Instant Pot. Now, spritz the bottom and sides of a baking pan with a nonstick cooking spray.

2. Add bread to the prepared pan. Top with fresh blackberries.

3. In a mixing bowl, thoroughly combine the cheese, honey, eggs, cinnamon, nutmeg, milk, and applesauce.

4. Pour this mixture into the pan, pressing the bread down with a wide spatula. Cut in cold butter. Now, cover the pan with a few paper towels.

5. Secure the lid. Choose the "Manual" mode. Cook for 20 minutes at High pressure. Once cooking is complete, use a natural release; carefully remove the lid.

6. Let cool completely.

Storing

1. Place a sheet of wax paper between each slice of French toast and place them in airtight containers; store in your refrigerator for up 1 to 2 days.

2. To freeze, place a sheet of wax paper between each slice of French toast. Wrap them tightly in foil or place in a heavy-duty freezer bag. Use within 1 to 2 months. Bon appétit!

17. Applesauce with a Healthy Twist

6 Servings

Ready in about
15 minutes

PER SERVING:
101 Calories; 0.2g Fat;
26.1g Carbs; 0.4g Protein;
20.4g Sugars

Forget a store-bought applesauce! This homemade applesauce is so easy to make in the Instant Pot and you won't be able to resist that flavor.

Ingredients

- 2 pounds cooking apples, peeled, cored and diced
- 1 ¼ cups water
- 1/4 cup orange juice

- 1 vanilla bean, split lengthwise
- 1 cinnamon stick
- 3 tablespoons date sugar

Directions

1. Add all ingredients to your Instant Pot.

2. Secure the lid. Choose the "Manual" mode. Cook for 8 minutes at High pressure. Once cooking is complete, use a quick release; carefully remove the lid

3. Next, allow the applesauce to cool completely. Afterwards, transfer your applesauce to jars. Let cool completely.

Storing

1. Spoon your applesauce into airtight containers; keep in the refrigerator for 1 to 2 weeks.

2. To freeze, spoon your applesauce into airtight containers. Freeze up to 1 to 2 months. Defrost in the refrigerator. Enjoy!

18. Cashew Porridge with Banana and Seeds

4 Servings

Ready in about
10 minutes

PER SERVING:
468 Calories; 31.7g Fat;
43.6g Carbs; 9.5g Protein;
26.8g Sugars

A warm and satisfying porridge is a perfect start to your day. Use fresh or dried fruits according to your taste. If you are going vegan, use a coconut oil and maple syrup.

Ingredients

- 1 cup raw cashews
- 1 ½ tablespoons raw sunflower seeds
- 2 tablespoons raw pumpkin seeds
- 1 cup almonds
- 1/2 teaspoon ground cinnamon
- 1/2 teaspoon ground cloves

- 2 cups water
- 1/2 stick butter
- 4 tablespoons honey
- 2 bananas, peeled and sliced
- A few drizzles of lemon juice

Directions

1. Pulse cashews, sunflower seeds, pumpkin seeds, and almonds in your food processor until the mixture resembles a coarse meal.

2. Transfer the mixture to the Instant Pot. Add cinnamon, cloves, water, butter, and honey. Secure the lid.

3. Choose "Manual" mode, High pressure and 5 minutes. Once cooking is complete, use a quick release; carefully remove the lid.

4. Top with banana slices. Drizzle banana slices with fresh lemon juice to prevent them from browning. Let cool completely.

Storing

1. Spoon your porridge into four airtight containers; keep in your refrigerator for up to 1 to 2 days.

2. For freezing, place your porridge in airtight containers or heavy-duty freezer bags. It will maintain the best quality for about 3 months. Defrost in the refrigerator.

19. MINI FRITTATA DI FORMAGGIO

4 Servings

Ready in about
40 minutes

PER SERVING:
490 Calories; 38.6g Fat;
9.1g Carbs; 26.4g Protein;
1.4g Sugars

Are you excited to discover more Instant Pot recipes? These mini frittatas are easy to make and fun to eat.

Ingredients

- 6 eggs, beaten
- 2 chorizo sausages, chopped
- 3/4 cup sour cream
- 1 cup scallions, chopped
- Sea salt, to taste
- 1 teaspoon garlic powder

- 1 teaspoon fennel seeds
- 1/2 teaspoon lemon pepper
- 2 tablespoons fresh basil, snipped
- 1 ¼ cups Colby cheese, shredded
- 4 tablespoons fresh parsley leaves, roughly chopped

Directions

1. Thoroughly combine the eggs, sausages, sour cream, scallions, salt, garlic powder, fennel seeds, lemon pepper, and fresh basil in a mixing bowl.

2. Pour the mixture into individual baking molds. Add 1 ½ cups of water and a metal trivet to the Instant Pot.

3. Place baking molds on the trivet. Secure the lid and choose "Manual" mode.

4. Cook at High pressure for 18 minutes. Once cooking is complete, use a natural release for 15 minutes; remove the lid carefully.

5. Scatter shredded Colby cheese on top of each mold; place under a preheated broiler for 6 minutes or until cheese is lightly browned. Garnish with fresh parsley leaves. Let cool completely.

Storing

1. Place mini frittatas in airtight containers; place in the refrigerator for up 3 to 4 days.

2. To freeze, place in separate Ziploc bags and freeze up to 3 months. Reheat in your microwave for a few minutes. Enjoy!

20. Potato Balls with Blue Cheese

10 Servings

Ready in about
1 hour 5 minutes

PER SERVING:
200 Calories; 10.6g Fat;
19.7g Carbs; 7.1g Protein;
1.8g Sugars

Blue cheese and potato balls are a delicious and impressive appetizer for a fancy dinner party or a girls' night in. Sweet potatoes cook perfectly in the Instant Pot.

Ingredients

- 2 pounds sweet potatoes, peeled and diced
- 1 onion, chopped
- 1 garlic clove, minced
- Sea salt and ground black pepper, to taste
- 1 teaspoon dried marjoram
- 1 teaspoon basil
- 1/2 teaspoon ground allspice
- 1/2 stick butter, softened
- 1 cup blue cheese, crumbled
- 2 eggs, whisked
- 2/3 cup breadcrumbs

Directions

1. Prepare your Instant Pot by adding 1 ½ cups of water and a metal trivet to its bottom. Lower sweet potatoes onto the trivet.

2. Secure the lid. Choose the "Manual" mode and cook for 15 minutes under High pressure. Once cooking is complete, use a natural release; carefully remove the lid.

3. Peel and mash the prepared sweet potatoes with the onion, garlic, and all of the seasonings. Now, stir in softened butter, cheese, and eggs.

4. Place this mixture in your refrigerator for 30 minutes; then, shape into bite-sized balls.

5. Coat each ball with breadcrumbs. Now, sprits the balls with a nonstick cooking spray. Bake the balls in the preheated oven at 425 degrees F approximately 15 minutes. Let cool completely.

Storing

1. Divide these balls between airtight containers or Ziploc bags; keep in your refrigerator for up to 3 to 4 days.

2. For freezing, place these balls in airtight containers. Freeze up to 1 month. Defrost in the refrigerator. Bon appétit!

LUNCH

21. ITALIAN-STYLE TOMATO SOUP

4 Servings

Ready in about
30 minutes

PER SERVING:
175 Calories; 11.1g Fat;
12.5g Carbs; 7.7g Protein;
6.7g Sugars

A thick, flavorful and Italian-inspired tomato soup is super easy to prepare in your Instant Pot. It is loaded with fiber and lycopene and gets an extra boost of flavor from a double cream.

Ingredients

- 1 tablespoon olive oil
- A bunch of scallions, chopped
- 1 garlic clove, minced
- 2 carrots, grated
- 1 celery, chopped
- 1 pounds tomatoes, seeded and chopped
- 4 cups roasted-vegetable broth

- Sea salt, to taste
- 1/4 teaspoon freshly ground black pepper
- 1/2 teaspoon cayenne pepper
- 1/2 teaspoon dried basil
- 1/2 teaspoon dried oregano
- 1/2 cup double cream
- 1 tablespoon fresh Italian parsley, roughly chopped

Directions

1. Press the "Sauté" button to heat up the Instant Pot. Now, heat the oil; sauté the scallions, garlic, carrot, and celery approximately 5 minutes.

2. Stir in the tomatoes, broth, salt, black pepper, cayenne pepper, basil, and oregano.

3. Secure the lid. Select the "Soup" setting; cook for 20 minutes at High pressure. Once cooking is complete, use a natural pressure release; carefully remove the lid.

4. Fold in the cream and purée the soup with an immersion blender. Top with fresh parsley.

5. Let cool completely.

Storing

1. Spoon the soup into four airtight containers; keep in your refrigerator for up to 4 days.

2. For freezing, place the soup in heavy-duty freezer bags. When the bags are frozen through, stack them up like file folders to save space in the freezer.

3. Freeze up to 4 months. Defrost in the microwave or refrigerator. Bon appétit!

22. QUICK AND EASY TURKEY CHILI

4 Servings

Ready in about
25 minutes

PER SERVING:
484 Calories; 29.3g
Fat; 14.1g Carbs; 41.5g
Protein; 4.4g Sugars

Your next go-to chili recipe! If you are in a hurry, you can skip searing the ground turkey and just add it to the Instant Pot with the remaining ingredients

Ingredients

- 1 tablespoon olive oil
- 2 garlic cloves, finely minced
- 1/2 cup shallots, finely chopped
- 1 carrot, sliced
- 1 bell pepper, chopped
- 1 jalapeno pepper, chopped
- 1 pound ground turkey

- 1 cup chicken bone broth
- 6 ounces beer
- 1 tablespoon cacao powder
- 1 tablespoon apple butter
- 1 teaspoon dried basil
- 1 (14-ounce) can tomatoes
- 1 (14-ounce) can kidney beans, drained and rinsed

Directions

1. Press the "Sauté" button to heat up your Instant Pot. Then, heat the oil; cook garlic, shallot, carrot, and bell peppers for about 5 minutes.

2. Stir in the ground turkey and cook for 3 minutes more, crumbling with a fork.

3. Secure the lid. Choose the "Poultry" setting and cook for 5 minutes under High pressure. Once cooking is complete, use a quick pressure release; carefully remove the lid. Let cool completely.

Storing

1. Spoon your chili into four airtight containers or Ziploc bags; keep in your refrigerator for up to 3 to 4 days.

2. For freezing, place your chili in airtight containers. It will maintain the best quality for about 4 to 6 months. Defrost in the refrigerator. Bon appétit!

23. ULTIMATE SLOPPY JOE

6 Servings

Ready in about
15 minutes

PER SERVING:
329 Calories; 23.3g Fat;
3.2g Carbs; 25.1g Protein;
1.7g Sugars

Comforting and full of flavor, Sloppy Joe is the perfect weekday autumn meal.
Could it be any more vintage?

Ingredients

- 1 tablespoon olive oil
- 1 pound ground chicken
- 1/2 pound ground pork
- 2 garlic cloves, minced
- 1 yellow onion, chopped
- 2 tomatoes, chopped

- 1 cup chicken broth
- Sea salt and ground black pepper, to taste
- 1/2 teaspoon paprika
- 1/2 teaspoon porcini powder
- 1/2 teaspoon fennel seeds
- 2 bay leaves

Directions

1. Press the "Sauté" button to heat up your Instant Pot; heat the oil. Now, cook the ground meat until it is delicately browned; reserve.

2. Sauté the garlic and onion in pan drippings for 2 to 3 minutes. Stir in the remaining ingredients.

3. Now, secure the lid. Choose the "Poultry" setting and cook for 5 minutes under High pressure.

4. Once cooking is complete, use a natural pressure release; carefully remove the lid. Let cool completely.

Storing

1. Place the meat mixture in airtight containers or Ziploc bags; keep in your refrigerator for up to 3 to 4 days.

2. For freezing, place the meat mixture in airtight containers or heavy-duty freezer bags. Freeze up to 2 to 3 months. Defrost in the refrigerator. Bon appétit!

24. Meatballs with Port Sauce

6 Servings

Ready in about
15 minutes

PER SERVING:
412 Calories; 23.1g Fat;
21.2g Carbs; 26g Protein;
7.2g Sugars

Here are elegant and flavorsome chicken-bacon meatballs for the perfect family lunch. Serve these irresistible balls over hot rice.

Ingredients

- 1 ¼ pounds ground chicken
- 4 slices bacon, chopped
- 1 cup seasoned breadcrumbs
- 1 onion, finely chopped
- 3 garlic cloves, minced
- 1/2 tablespoon fresh rosemary, finely chopped
- 2 eggs, beaten

- Salt and ground black pepper, to taste
- 1/2 teaspoon paprika
- 2 tablespoons olive oil
- 2 cups tomato purée
- 2 tablespoons Dijon mustard
- 1 tablespoon Worcestershire sauce
- 2 tablespoons ruby port
- 1/4 cup chicken broth

Directions

1. Thoroughly combine the ground chicken, bacon, breadcrumbs, onion, garlic, rosemary, eggs, salt, black pepper, and paprika.

2. Shape the mixture into meatballs and reserve.

3. Press the "Sauté" button on High heat to preheat your Instant Pot. Heat olive oil and sear the meatballs until they are browned on all sides; work in batches.

4. Add the other ingredients. Choose the "Manual" setting and cook at High pressure for 7 minutes. Use a quick pressure release and carefully remove the lid. Let cool completely.

Storing

1. Place meatballs in airtight containers or Ziploc bags; keep in your refrigerator for up to 3 to 4 days.

2. Freeze the meatballs in airtight containers or heavy-duty freezer bags. Freeze up to 3 to 4 months. To defrost, slowly reheat in a saucepan. Bon appétit!

25. Colorful Chicken Soup

5 Servings

Ready in about
25 minutes

PER SERVING:
238 Calories; 17g Fat; 5.4g
Carbs; 16.4g Protein; 2.6g
Sugars

Here's a rich, colorful and nourishing chicken soup your family will love for sure!
Rose wine is the perfect addition that compliments this chicken dish.

Ingredients

- 2 tablespoons olive oil
- 1 pound chicken drumettes
- 1 yellow onion, chopped
- 2 cloves garlic, minced
- 1 red bell peppers, seeded and sliced
- 1 green bell pepper, seeded and sliced
- 1 orange bell pepper, seeded and sliced
- 1 carrot, thinly sliced

- 1 parsnip, thinly sliced
- 1/4 cup Rose wine
- Sea salt and ground black pepper, to your liking
- 1/2 teaspoon dried dill
- 1/2 teaspoon dried oregano
- 1 tablespoon granulated chicken bouillon
- 4 cups water

Directions

1. Press the "Sauté" button to heat up your Instant Pot; now, heat the oil until sizzling. Then, sauté the onion and garlic until tender and fragrant.

2. Add the peppers, carrots and parsnip; cook an additional 3 minutes or until the vegetables are softened. Add a splash of rose wine to deglaze the bottom of your Instant Pot.

3. Then, stir in the remaining ingredients; stir to combine well.

4. Secure the lid. Choose the "Soup" mode and High pressure; cook for 20 minutes. Once cooking is complete, use a quick pressure release. Carefully remove the lid.

5. Remove the chicken wings from the cooking liquid; discard the bones and chop the meat. Add the chicken meat back to the Instant Pot and stir. Let cool completely.

Storing

1. Spoon the soup into airtight containers or Ziploc bags; keep in your refrigerator for up to 3 to 4 days.

2. For freezing, place the soup in airtight containers. It will maintain the best quality for about 4 to 6 months. Defrost in the refrigerator. Bon appétit!

26. Easy Peppery Pork Steaks

6 Servings

Ready in about
15 minutes

PER SERVING:
476 Calories; 44.2g Fat;
0.1g Carbs; 21.2g Protein;
0.1g Sugars

A great pork steak is not just about the recipe. It's also about the reliable cooker.
You could also try adding some chili peppers to give this pork an extra kick.

Ingredients

- 2 teaspoons lard
- 1 ½ pounds pork steaks
- 1 cup roasted vegetable broth
- 2 sprigs rosemary

- 1 sprig thyme
- 1 tablespoon fresh parsley
- Salt, to taste
- 1/2 teaspoon mixed peppercorns

Directions

1. Press the "Sauté" button to preheat your Instant Pot; melt the lard. Once hot, sear the pork until delicately browned.

2. Stir in the remaining ingredients.

3. Secure the lid. Choose the "Manual" setting and cook at High pressure for 8 minutes. Once cooking is complete, use a quick pressure release; carefully remove the lid.

4. Press the "Sauté" button to thicken the sauce. Let cool completely.

Storing

1. Place the steaks in airtight containers or Ziploc bags; keep in your refrigerator for up to 3 to 4 days.

2. For freezing, place the steaks in airtight containers or heavy-duty freezer bags. Freeze up to 2 to 3 months. Defrost in the refrigerator. Bon appétit!

27. PORK STEW WITH SOUR CREAM

5 Servings

Ready in about
15 minutes

PER SERVING:
279 Calories; 10.1g Fat;
18.1g Carbs; 30g Protein;
8.2g Sugars

Your family will ever guess that this stew has not cooked all afternoon. Habanero pepper can lower your cholesterol and blood pressure as well as protect against prostate cancer.

Ingredients

- 2 teaspoons olive oil
- 1 pound pork stew meat, cubed
- 1 cup tomato paste
- 2 tablespoons fresh cilantro, chopped
- 2 tablespoons fresh parsley, chopped
- 1 leek, chopped
- 1 habanero pepper, deveined and minced

- 1 teaspoon ginger-garlic paste
- 1 teaspoon ground cumin
- 1 teaspoon paprika
- Kosher salt and black pepper, to taste
- 5 cups beef bone broth
- 1 cup sour cream, for garnish

Directions

1. Press the "Sauté" button to preheat your Instant Pot; heat the oil. Now, sear the meat until it is delicately browned.

2. Add tomato paste, cilantro, parsley, leek, habanero pepper, ginger-garlic paste, cumin, paprika, salt, black pepper, and broth.

3. Secure the lid. Choose the "Manual" setting and cook at High pressure for 8 minutes. Once cooking is complete, use a quick pressure release; carefully remove the lid.

4. Top with sour cream. Let cool completely.

Storing

1. Spoon the stew into airtight containers or Ziploc bags; keep in your refrigerator for up to 3 to 4 days.

2. For freezing, place the stew in airtight containers. Freeze up to 4 to 6 months. Defrost in the refrigerator. Bon appétit!

28. GREEN BEANS AND PANCETTA DELIGHT

4 Servings

Ready in about
10 minutes

PER SERVING:
177 Calories; 12.1g Fat;
9.9g Carbs; 8.8g Protein;
2.3g Sugars

Your family will love a fresh and rich taste of this dish. Add a few sprinkles of pumpkin seeds just before serving!

Ingredients

- 2 tablespoons sesame oil
- 2 garlic cloves, pressed
- 1 yellow onion, chopped
- 5 ounces pancetta, diced
- 1 ½ pounds green beans, cut in half
- Kosher salt, to taste

- 1/4 teaspoon ground black pepper
- 1/2 teaspoon cayenne pepper
- 1/2 teaspoon dried oregano
- 1/2 teaspoon dried dill
- 1 cup water

Directions

1. Press the "Sauté" button to heat up your Instant Pot. Now, heat the sesame oil and sauté the garlic and onion until softened and fragrant; set it aside.

2. After that, stir in pancetta and continue to cook for a further 4 minutes; crumble with a fork and set it aside.

3. Add the remaining ingredients; stir to combine.

4. Secure the lid. Choose the "Manual" mode and Low pressure; cook for 3 minutes. Once cooking is complete, use a quick pressure release; carefully remove the lid.

5. Add the reserved onion/garlic mixture and pancetta. Let cool completely.

Storing

1. Divide the mixture into four portions; divide the portions between four airtight containers; keep in your refrigerator for up 3 to 5 days.

2. For freezing, place the mixture in airtight containers. Freeze up to 10 to 12 months. Defrost in the refrigerator. Bon appétit!

29. Beef Steak with Rum Sauce

6 Servings

Ready in about
25 minutes

PER SERVING:
293 Calories; 15.6g Fat;
4.3g Carbs; 27.3g Protein;
0.9g Sugars

Whether you are planning an elegant dinner party or Sunday family lunch, this saucy beef makes the perfect main dish. Serve over spaghetti.

Ingredients

- 2 tablespoons olive oil
- 1 ½ pounds beef flank steak
- Sea salt and freshly ground black pepper, to taste
- 1 teaspoon cayenne pepper
- 1 teaspoon dried marjoram
- 1/2 teaspoon dried thyme

- 1/2 teaspoon dried basil
- 1/4 cup white rum
- 1 cup water
- 2 bell peppers, deveined and chopped
- 1 Chile de Arbol, deveined and minced
- 1 shallot, halved and sliced
- 1 cup sour cream

Directions

1. Press the "Sauté" button to preheat your Instant Pot. Then, heat the oil until sizzling. Once hot, cook the beef until browned on all sides.

2. Add seasonings. Deglaze the inner pot with white rum and add water, peppers, and shallot.

3. Secure the lid. Choose the "Poultry" setting and cook at High pressure for 15 minutes. Once cooking is complete, use a quick pressure release; carefully remove the lid.

4. Transfer the meat to a cutting board; slice the beef against the grain.

5. Now, fold in sour cream and press the "Sauté" button; let it simmer until the cooking liquid is thoroughly warmed and reduced. Let cool completely.

Storing

1. Spoon the beef along with the sauce into airtight containers; keep in your refrigerator for 3 to 4 days.

2. For freezing, place the beef along with the sauce in airtight containers or heavy-duty freezer bags. Freeze up to 2 to 3 months. Defrost in the microwave. Bon appétit!

30. TRADITIONAL AUTUMN DISH (SATARASH)

6 Servings

Ready in about
35 minutes

PER SERVING:
403 Calories; 21.3g
Fat; 16.4g Carbs; 36.8g
Protein; 8.7g Sugars

A hearty stew that will nourish and energize your body and soul. This traditional dish can be served in less than 35 minutes. Amazing!

Ingredients

- 1 tablespoon olive oil
- 2 pounds beef sirloin steak, cut into bite-sized chunks
- 1 cup red onion, chopped
- 2 garlic cloves, minced
- 1 pound bell peppers, seeded and sliced

- 1 cup vegetable broth
- 4 Italian plum tomatoes, crushed
- Salt and ground black pepper, to taste
- 1 teaspoon paprika
- 1 egg, beaten

Directions

1. Press the "Sauté" button to preheat your Instant Pot. Now, heat the oil. Cook the beef until it is no longer pink.

2. Add onion and cook an additional 2 minutes. Stir in the minced garlic, peppers, broth, tomatoes, salt, black pepper, and paprika.

3. Secure the lid. Choose the "Soup" mode and High pressure; cook for 20 minutes. Once cooking is complete, use a quick pressure release; carefully remove the lid.

4. Afterwards, fold in the egg and stir well; seal the lid and let it sit in the residual heat for 8 to 10 minutes.

5. Let cool completely.

Storing

1. Spoon the stew into airtight containers or Ziploc bags; keep in your refrigerator for up to 3 to 4 days.

2. For freezing, place the stew in airtight containers. Freeze up to 4 to 6 months. Defrost in the refrigerator. Bon appétit!

31. FANCY TACO BOWLS

4 Servings

Ready in about
15 minutes

PER SERVING:
409 Calories; 15.7g
Fat; 37.5g Carbs; 29.5g
Protein; 6.6g Sugars

You can make your own homemade taco bowls using the underside of a muffin tin and store-bought corn tortillas. Garnish with ripe black olives and reduced-fat sour cream, if desired.

Ingredients

- 1 tablespoon peanut oil
- 1 pound ground chuck
- 1 cup beef bone broth
- 1 bell pepper, seeded and chopped
- 1 red chili pepper, seeded and chopped

- 1 onion, chopped
- 1 (1.25-ounce) package taco seasoning
- 4 tortilla bowls, baked
- 1 (15-ounce) can beans, drained and rinsed
- 2 fresh tomatoes, chopped

Directions

1. Press the "Sauté" button and preheat the Instant Pot. Heat the oil and cook the ground chuck until it is no longer pink.

2. Add the broth, bell pepper, chili pepper, onion, and taco seasoning.

3. Secure the lid. Choose the "Manual" mode and High pressure; cook for 5 minutes. Once cooking is complete, use a quick pressure release; carefully remove the lid.

4. Top with beans and tomatoes. Let cool completely.

Storing

1. Place the ground beef mixture in airtight containers; keep in your refrigerator for 3 to 4 days.

2. Freeze the ground beef mixture in airtight containers or heavy-duty freezer bags. Freeze up to 2 to 3 months. Defrost them in the refrigerator and reheat in the microwave.

3. Cover tortilla bowls with foil to prevent drying out; keep in the refrigerator for 1 to 2 days.

4. For freezing, wrap tortillas tightly in foil; freeze up to 2 months. Enjoy!

32. FISH STEW WITH HERBS

4 Servings

Ready in about
15 minutes

PER SERVING:
221 Calories; 9.3g Fat;
4.9g Carbs; 25g Protein;
1.8g Sugars

This fish stew is made delicious in no time thanks to the Instant Pot. If you like spicy food, feel free to add a few serrano peppers to the stew.

Ingredients

- 2 tablespoons sesame oil
- 1 cup scallions, chopped
- 2 garlic cloves, minced
- 1/3 cup dry vermouth
- 1 cup shellfish stock
- 2 cups water
- 2 ripe plum tomatoes, crushed
- Sea salt, to taste

- 1/4 teaspoon freshly ground black pepper, or more to taste
- 1 teaspoon hot paprika
- 1 pound tilapia fillets, boneless, skinless and diced
- 1 tablespoon fresh lime juice
- 1 teaspoon dried rosemary
- 1/2 teaspoon dried oregano
- 1/2 teaspoon dried basil

Directions

1. Press the "Sauté" button to preheat your Instant Pot. Heat the oil and sauté the scallions and garlic until fragrant.

2. Add a splash of vermouth to deglaze the bottom of the inner pot.

3. Secure the lid. Choose the "Manual" mode and High pressure; cook for 5 minutes. Once cooking is complete, use a quick pressure release; carefully remove the lid. Let cool completely.

Storing

1. Spoon the stew into airtight containers or Ziploc bags; keep in your refrigerator for up to 3 to 4 days.

2. For freezing, place the stew in airtight containers. Freeze up to 4 to 6 months. Defrost in the refrigerator. Bon appétit!

33. INDIAN-STYLE HADDOCK FILLETS

4 Servings

Ready in about
15 minutes

PER SERVING:
273 Calories; 9.3g Fat;
13.5g Carbs; 34.9g
Protein; 6.6g Sugars

This is a traditional, creamy and aromatic Indian dish also known as Tikka masala.
Serve with warm naan and lots of fresh salad.

Ingredients

- 2 tablespoons olive oil
- 1/2 cup scallions, chopped
- 2 garlic cloves, minced
- 1/4 cup tikka masala curry paste
- 1/3 teaspoon ground allspice
- 1 (14-ounce) can diced tomatoes

- 1 tablespoon brown sugar
- 1 teaspoon hot paprika
- 1 cup vegetable broth
- 1 ½ pounds haddock fillets, cut into bite-sized chunks
- 1 cup natural yogurt
- 1 lime, cut into wedges

Directions

1. Press the "Sauté" button to preheat your Instant Pot; heat the oil. Then, sauté the scallions until tender and translucent.

2. Now, add the garlic; continue to sauté for a further 30 seconds.

3. Stir curry paste, allspice, tomatoes, sugar, paprika, broth, and haddock into the Instant Pot.

4. Secure the lid and choose the "Manual" setting. Cook for 5 minutes at Low pressure. Once cooking is complete, use a quick release; carefully remove the lid.

5. Then, fold in natural yogurt and stir to combine well; seal the lid again and allow it to sit in the residual heat until warmed through.

6. Garnish with lime wedges. Let cool completely.

Storing

1. Spoon your dish into airtight containers; it will last for 3 to 4 days in the refrigerator.

2. For freezing, place your dish in airtight containers or heavy-duty freezer bags. Freeze up to 4 to 6 months. Defrost in the microwave or refrigerator. Bon appétit!

34. Hungarian Paprika Fisherman's Stew (Halászlé)

4 Servings

Ready in about
15 minutes

PER SERVING:
310 Calories; 13.7g
Fat; 14.4g Carbs; 32.3g
Protein; 4.5g Sugars

Are you looking for a recipe for a relaxed lunch with your family? Look no further!
This authentic one-pot meal will be ready in no time.

Ingredients

- 2 tablespoons butter, at room temperature
- 1 cup leeks, chopped
- 2 bell peppers, seeded and sliced
- 2 garlic cloves, minced
- 2 sprigs thyme
- 1 sprig rosemary
- 1 teaspoon sweet paprika
- 1 teaspoon hot paprika
- Sea salt and ground black pepper, to taste

- 2 tomatoes, puréed
- 2 cups vegetable broth
- 2 cups water
- 1 ½ pounds cod fish, cut into bite-sized chunks
- 2 tablespoons fresh cilantro, roughly chopped
- 1 cup sour cream, well-chilled

Directions

1. Press the "Sauté" button to preheat your Instant Pot. Melt the butter and sauté the leeks until fragrant.

2. Then, stir in the peppers and garlic and continue to sauté an additional 40 seconds.

3. Add thyme, rosemary, paprika, salt, black pepper, tomatoes, broth, water, and fish.

4. Secure the lid and choose the "Manual" setting. Cook for 6 minutes at High pressure. Once cooking is complete, use a quick release; carefully remove the lid.

5. Garnish with fresh cilantro and well-chilled sour cream. Let cool completely.

Storing

1. Spoon Halászlé into airtight containers or Ziploc bags; keep in your refrigerator for up to 3 to 4 days.

2. For freezing, place Halászlé in airtight containers. Freeze up to 4 to 6 months. Defrost in the refrigerator. Bon appétit!

35. RICE WITH SAUSAGE AND OLIVES

4 Servings

Ready in about
20 minutes

PER SERVING:
576 Calories; 34.7g
Fat; 44.8g Carbs; 20.5g
Protein; 2.3g Sugars

If your family love rice and sausage, the Instant Pot is a great tool to prepare this all-in-one meal while saving you time in the kitchen.

Ingredients

- 2 tablespoons butter, melted
- 1 yellow onion, chopped
- 2 carrots, trimmed and chopped
- 1/2 pound Chorizo sausage, sliced
- 1 cup white long-grain rice

- 2 cups chicken stock
- Sea salt and ground black pepper, to taste
- 1/4 cup lightly packed fresh coriander, roughly chopped
- 1 cup black olives, pitted and sliced

Directions

1. Press the "Sauté" button to preheat your Instant Pot. Now, melt the butter and cook the onion until aromatic.

2. Then, add the carrot and Chorizo; cook an additional 2 minutes. Add the remaining ingredients and stir to combine well.

3. Secure the lid. Choose the "Manual" mode and High pressure; cook for 3 minutes. Once cooking is complete, use a natural pressure release for 10 minutes; carefully remove the lid.

4. Let cool completely.

Storing

1. Spoon your rice into airtight containers or Ziploc bags; keep in your refrigerator for up to 4 to 6 days.

2. For freezing, place your rice in airtight containers. Freeze up to 6 months. Defrost in the refrigerator. Bon appétit!

36. Quick and Easy Navy Beans

6 Servings

Ready in about
35 minutes

PER SERVING:
292 Calories; 1.6g Fat;
52.3g Carbs; 19g Protein;
3.6g Sugars

Navy beans are a great source of dietary fiber, iron, phosphorus, B1, manganese, copper, and protein.

Ingredients

- 1 ¼ pounds dry navy beans
- 6 cups water
- 2 tablespoons bouillon granules
- 2 bay leaves
- 1 teaspoon black peppercorns, to taste

Directions

1. Rinse off and drain navy beans. Place navy beans, water, bouillon granules, bay leaves, and black peppercorns in your Instant Pot.

2. Secure the lid. Choose the "Manual" mode and cook at High pressure for 20 minutes.

3. Once cooking is complete, use a natural release; remove the lid carefully. Let cool completely.

Storing

1. Spoon your beans into airtight containers or Ziploc bags; keep in your refrigerator for up to 3 to 4 days.

2. For freezing, place your beans in airtight containers. It will maintain the best quality for about 4 to 6 months. Defrost in the refrigerator. Bon appétit!

37. Curried Cabbage with Root Vegetables

4 Servings

Ready in about
20 minutes

PER SERVING:
223 Calories; 8.2g Fat;
33.8g Carbs; 7.6g Protein;
15.1g Sugars

Here's an amazing cabbage recipe that you would never dream of making. This curry cabbage is delicious served with hot cooked rice and a pickled salad.

Ingredients

- 2 tablespoons olive oil
- 1 medium-sized leek, chopped
- 2 cloves garlic, smashed
- 1 ½ pounds white cabbage, shredded
- 1 cup vegetable broth
- 1 cup tomatoes, puréed
- 1 parsnip, chopped
- 2 carrots, chopped
- 2 stalks celery, chopped
- 1 turnip, chopped
- 1/2 tablespoon fresh lime juice
- 1 teaspoon dried basil
- 1/2 teaspoon dried dill
- 1 teaspoon ground coriander
- 1 teaspoon ground turmeric
- 1 bay leaf
- Kosher salt and ground black pepper, to taste
- 1 (14-ounce) can coconut milk

Directions

1. Press the "Sauté" button to preheat your Instant Pot. Now, heat the oil and cook the leeks and garlic until tender and fragrant.

2. After that, add the remaining ingredients; stir to combine well.

3. Secure the lid. Choose the "Manual" mode and cook for 12 minutes under High pressure. Once cooking is complete, use a natural release; carefully remove the lid. Let cool completely.

Storing

1. Place the cabbage in airtight containers or Ziploc bags; keep in your refrigerator for 3 to 5 days.

2. Place the cabbage in freezable containers; they can be frozen for up to 10 months. Defrost in the refrigerator or microwave. Bon appétit!

38. Spicy Peppery Millet

4 Servings

Ready in about
20 minutes

PER SERVING:
339 Calories; 6.6g Fat;
60.6g Carbs; 9.2g Protein;
2.9g Sugars

This is one of the most common ways to eat millet. Prepare this savory porridge in no time and enjoy with your family!

Ingredients

- 1 tablespoon olive oil
- 1 red onion, chopped
- 1 red bell pepper, deveined and sliced
- 1 green bell pepper, deveined and sliced
- 1 ancho chili pepper, deveined and chopped

- 1/2 teaspoon granulated garlic
- 1 teaspoon salt
- 1/4 teaspoon ground black pepper
- 1/4 teaspoon cayenne pepper
- 1 ½ cups millet
- 3 cups water

Directions

1. Press the "Sauté" button to preheat your Instant Pot. Then, heat the oil until sizzling; sauté the onions until they are caramelized.

2. Stir in the peppers and continue to sauté an additional 2 minutes or until they are tender and fragrant.

3. Add granulated garlic, salt, black pepper, cayenne pepper, millet, and water.

4. Secure the lid. Choose the "Manual" mode and High pressure; cook for 5 minutes. Once cooking is complete, use a natural pressure release for 10 minutes; carefully remove the lid.

5. Lastly, fluff the millet with a fork. Let cool completely.

Storing

1. Place the millet in airtight containers or Ziploc bags; keep in your refrigerator for 3 to 5 days.

2. Place the millet in freezable containers; they can be frozen for up to 1 month. Defrost in the refrigerator or microwave. Bon appétit!

39. PILAF WITH CREMINI MUSHROOMS

5 Servings

Ready in about
15 minutes

PER SERVING:
335 Calories; 14.9g Fat;
60g Carbs; 11g Protein;
2.3g Sugars

Cremini mushrooms are a powerhouse of Vitamin B-complex, zinc, potassium, selenium, phosphorus and manganese.

Ingredients

- 2 cups jasmine rice
- 2 cups water
- 1/4 teaspoon kosher salt
- 2 tablespoons butter

- 1 onion, chopped
- 2 garlic cloves, minced
- 1/2 pound Cremini mushrooms, thinly sliced

Directions

1. Rinse rice under cold running water and transfer to the Instant Pot; add water and 1/4 teaspoon of salt.

2. Secure the lid and select the "Manual" mode. Cook at High pressure for 6 minutes. Once cooking is complete, use a natural release; remove the lid carefully.

3. Fluff rice with the rice paddle or fork; reserve.

4. Press the "Sauté" button and melt the butter. Now, sauté the onion until tender and translucent. Add garlic and cook an additional minute or until it is fragrant and lightly browned.

5. Add Cremini mushrooms and continue to sauté until they are slightly browned. Add reserved jasmine rice and stir. Let cool completely.

Storing

1. Spoon your pilaf into airtight containers or Ziploc bags; keep in your refrigerator for up to 4 to 6 days.

2. For freezing, place your pilaf in airtight containers. Freeze up to 6 months. Defrost in the refrigerator. Bon appétit!

40. Saucy Chuck Roast

6 Servings

Ready in about
45 minutes

PER SERVING:
252 Calories; 9.9g Fat; 9g
Carbs; 30.1g Protein; 5.9g
Sugars

Here's a cheap, delicious and satisfying lunch. You can substitute beef broth for teriyaki sauce. Enjoy!

Ingredients

- 2 tablespoons lard, at room temperature
- 2 pounds chuck roast
- 4 carrots, sliced
- 1/2 cup leek, sliced
- 1 teaspoon garlic, minced

- 3 teaspoons fresh ginger root, thinly sliced
- Salt and pepper, to taste
- 1 ½ tablespoons fresh parsley leaves, roughly chopped
- 1 cup barbeque sauce
- 1/2 cup teriyaki sauce

Directions

1. Press the "Sauté" button on your Instant Pot. Now, melt the lard until hot.

2. Sear chuck roast until browned, about 6 minutes per side. Add the other ingredients.

3. Choose "Manual" setting and cook for 35 minutes at High pressure or until the internal temperature of the chuck roast is at least 145 degrees F.

4. Once cooking is complete, use a quick release; remove the lid. Let cool completely.

Storing

1. Place the chuck roast in airtight containers; keep in your refrigerator for 3 to 4 days.

2. For freezing, place the chuck roast in airtight containers or heavy-duty freezer bags. Freeze up to 2 to 3 months. Defrost in the refrigerator or microwave. Bon appétit!

DINNER

41. Mashed Cauliflower with Cheese and Beer

5 Servings

Ready in about
20 minutes

PER SERVING:
297 Calories; 23.6g Fat;
8.9g Carbs; 12.8g Protein;
1.4g Sugars

Cauliflower is one of the most versatile vegetables ever! Colby cheese and beer turn this simple mashed vegetable into a decadent side dish.

Ingredients

- 1 1/3 cups water
- 1 cauliflower head
- 1/2 teaspoon cayenne pepper
- Sea salt and freshly ground black pepper
- 2 tablespoons butter

- 1 ½ tablespoons arrowroot powder
- 1/2 cup beer
- 1 teaspoon garlic powder
- 1 ½ cup Colby cheese, shredded
- 1/2 cup sour cream

Directions

1. Add 1 1/3 cups of water to your Instant Pot.

2. Put the cauliflower head into the steaming basket. Transfer the steaming basket to the Instant Pot.

3. Secure the lid and choose the "Manual" button, High pressure and 5 minutes. Once cooking is complete, use a quick release; carefully remove the lid.

4. Season cooked cauliflower with cayenne pepper, salt, and ground black pepper. Mash cooked cauliflower with a potato masher.

5. Next, melt butter in a pan that is preheated over moderate heat. Whisk in the arrowroot powder and cook for 40 seconds, stirring continuously.

6. Gradually pour in beer, stirring continuously. Add the garlic powder and cook until the sauce has thickened, for 3 to 4 minutes.

7. Remove from heat and stir in Colby cheese and sour cream; stir until the cheese has melted. Add mashed cauliflower and stir until everything is well incorporated. Let cool completely.

Storing

1. Transfer the mashed cauliflower to the airtight containers and place in your refrigerator for up to 3 to 4 days.

2. For freezing, place the mashed cauliflower in freezer safe containers and freeze up to 1 month. Defrost in the microwave for a few minutes.

42. Garlicy Creamy Mashed Potatoes

4 Servings

Ready in about
15 minutes

PER SERVING:
230 Calories; 14g Fat;
23.3g Carbs; 3.8g Protein;
1.7g Sugars

Yukon Gold potatoes and spring onions are magically transformed into a creamy and flavorful supper that your family will love!

Ingredients

- 1 cup water
- 1 pound Yukon Gold potatoes, peeled and cubed
- 1/2 stick butter, softened
- 2 tablespoons spring garlic, minced
- 1/4 cup milk

- 1/3 cup sour cream
- 1/2 teaspoon dried oregano
- 1/2 teaspoon dried rosemary
- 1/2 teaspoon paprika
- Salt and ground black pepper, to taste

Directions

1. Add 1 cup of water and steamer basket to the base of your Instant Pot.

2. Place cubed potatoes in the steamer basket; transfer it to the Instant Pot. Secure the lid. Select the "Manual" mode; cook for 4 minutes under High pressure.

3. Once cooking is complete, use a quick release; carefully remove the lid.

4. Meanwhile, heat a pan over a moderate heat. Melt the butter and cook spring garlic until it is tender and aromatic.

5. Add the milk and scrape up any browned bits with a spatula. Allow it to cool slightly.

6. In a mixing bowl, mash the cooked potatoes. Add the butter/garlic mixture along with the other ingredients.

7. Taste and adjust the seasonings. Let cool completely.

Storing

1. Place mashed potatoes in airtight containers or Ziploc bags; keep in your refrigerator for 3 to 5 days.

2. Place mashed potatoes in freezable containers; it will maintain the best quality for 10 to 12 months. Defrost in the refrigerator or microwave. Bon appétit!

43. WINE-BRAISED CHICKEN

4 Servings

Ready in about
25 minutes

PER SERVING:
255 Calories; 12.1g Fat;
6.9g Carbs; 29.2g Protein;
2.7g Sugars

Earthy chestnut mushrooms, shallots, tomatoes, and aromatics make this amazingly juicy chicken dish. You can replace red wine with chicken broth and add two tablespoons of cognac.

Ingredients

- 2 teaspoons peanut oil
- 2 chicken drumettes
- 1 chicken breast
- 2 shallots, chopped
- 2 cloves garlic, crushed
- 1/2 pound chestnut mushrooms, halved
- 1 cup vegetable stock

- 1/3 cup red wine
- Sea salt and ground black pepper, to your liking
- 1/2 teaspoon red pepper flakes
- 1/4 teaspoon curry powder
- 1/4 cup tomato puree
- 2 teaspoons all-purpose flour
- 2 sprigs fresh thyme, leaves picked

Directions

1. Press the "Sauté" button and heat peanut oil. Add the chicken, skin-side down, and cook for 7 minutes or until browned; reserve.

2. Now, add the shallots and sauté until they're tender and fragrant. Now, stir in the garlic and mushrooms, and cook until aromatic.

3. Add 1/2 cup of vegetable stock and red wine, and scrape the bottom of your Instant Pot to loosen any stuck-on bits.

4. Add the salt, black pepper, red pepper flakes, and curry powder; continue to cook, stirring constantly.

5. Now, add the reserved chicken, tomato puree and the remaining 1/2 cup of vegetable stock. Sprinkle with all-purpose flour and fresh thyme leaves.

6. Secure the lid. Choose the "Manual" and cook at High pressure for 11 minutes. Once cooking is complete, use a quick pressure release; carefully remove the lid. Let cool completely.

Storing

1. Place the chicken mixture in airtight containers or Ziploc bags; keep in your refrigerator for 3 to 4 days.

2. For freezing, place them in airtight containers or heavy-duty freezer bags. It will maintain the best quality for about 4 months. Defrost in the refrigerator. Enjoy!

44. Fancy Chicken Cutlets

4 Servings

Ready in about
20 minutes

PER SERVING:
190 Calories; 8.4g Fat;
4.3g Carbs; 23.6g Protein;
2g Sugars

What could be better than pressure-cooked chicken cutlets topped with zingy, buttery sauce?! Serve with polenta or warm egg noodles.

Ingredients

- 1 pound chicken cutlets, pounded to 1/4-inch thickness
- 2 garlic cloves, peeled and halved
- 1/3 teaspoon salt
- Ground black pepper and cayenne pepper, to taste
- 2 teaspoons sesame oil
- 3/4 cup water

- 1 ½ tablespoons dry sherry
- 1 chicken bouillon cube
- 2 tablespoons fresh lime juice
- 1 teaspoon dried thyme
- 1 teaspoon dried marjoram
- 1 teaspoon mustard powder
- 3 teaspoons butter, softened

Directions

1. Rub the chicken with garlic halves; then, season with salt, black pepper, and cayenne pepper. Press the "Sauté" button.

2. Once hot, heat sesame oil and sauté chicken cutlets for 5 minutes, turning once during cooking. Add water and dry sherry and stir; scrape the bottom of the pan to deglaze.

3. Secure the lid. Choose the "Manual" mode and High pressure; cook for 4 minutes. Once cooking is complete, use a quick pressure release; carefully remove the lid. Reserve the chicken cutlets, keeping them warm.

4. Stir bouillon cube, lime juice, thyme, marjoram, and mustard powder into the cooking liquid.

5. Press the "Sauté" button and simmer for 6 minutes or until the cooking liquid has reduced and concentrated.

6. Add the butter to the sauce, stir to combine, and adjust the seasonings. Pour the prepared sauce over reserved chicken cutlets. Let cool completely.

Storing

1. Place chicken cutlets in airtight containers or Ziploc bags; keep in your refrigerator for 3 to 4 days.

2. For freezing, place them in airtight containers or heavy-duty freezer bags. It will maintain the best quality for about 4 months. Defrost in the refrigerator. Enjoy!

45. STUFFED TURKEY WITH CHEESE AND VEGETABLES

4 Servings

Ready in about
35 minutes

PER SERVING:
475 Calories; 25.4g Fat;
8.2g Carbs; 50g Protein;
2.9g Sugars

This classic turkey dish is elegant enough to serve for a festive Thanksgiving dinner but simple enough for an everyday lunch.

Ingredients

- 3 tablespoons olive oil
- 2 shallots, chopped
- 2 garlic cloves, smashed
- 1 carrot, chopped
- 1 parsnip, chopped
- 2 tablespoons fresh coriander, chopped
- Sea salt and freshly ground black pepper, to your liking
- 1 teaspoon paprika

- 1 cup dried bread flakes
- 1/2 teaspoon garlic powder
- 1/2 teaspoon cumin powder
- 1/3 teaspoon turmeric powder
- 2 ½ cups turkey stock, preferably homemade
- 4 ounces chèvre cheese
- 2 pounds turkey breast tenderloins

Directions

1. Press the "Sauté" button to preheat your Instant Pot. Now, heat 1 tablespoon of olive oil and sauté the shallots, garlic, carrot, and parsnip until they have softened.

2. Add coriander, salt, black pepper, paprika, dried bread flakes, garlic powder, cumin, and turmeric powder; stir to combine well.

3. Now, slowly and gradually pour in 1/2 cup of turkey stock. Add chèvre and mix to combine well.

4. Place the turkey breast on a work surface and spread the stuffing mixture over it. Tie a cotton kitchen string around each tenderloin.

5. Press the "Sauté' button on High heat.

6. Once hot, add the remaining 2 tablespoons of olive oil. Sear turkey about 4 minutes on each side. Add the remaining turkey stock and secure the lid.

7. Choose "Manual", High pressure and 25 minutes cooking time. Use a natural pressure release; carefully remove the lid. Transfer stuffed turkey tenderloins to a serving platter.

8. Press the "Sauté" button again and thicken the cooking liquid. Spoon the sauce over the stuffed turkey tenderloins. Let cool completely.

Storing

1. Wrap each turkey tenderloin in foil before packing them into an airtight container; keep in your refrigerator for up to 3 to 4 days.

2. For freezing, wrap each turkey tenderloin in foil before packing them into airtight containers or heavy-duty freezer bags. Freeze up to 3 months. Defrost in the refrigerator. Bon appétit!

46. DAD'S TURKEY MEATLOAF WITH CHEESE

8 Servings

Ready in about
35 minutes

PER SERVING:
387 Calories; 24g Fat; 5g
Carbs; 36.9g Protein; 1.7g
Sugars

This cheesy meatloaf is pressure cooked with tomato paste and Italian seasonings.
Comfort food at its finest.

Ingredients

- 1 ½ pounds ground turkey
- 1 pound ground pork
- 1 cup breadcrumbs
- 1 cup Romano cheese, grated
- 1 tablespoon Worcestershire sauce
- 1 egg, chopped
- Salt and ground black pepper, to taste

- 1/2 cup scallions, chopped
- 2 garlic cloves, minced
- 6 ounces tomatoes, puréed
- 2 tablespoons tomato ketchup
- 1/2 cup water
- 1 teaspoon Old Sub Sailor seasoning

Directions

1. Prepare your Instant Pot by adding a metal rack and 1 ½ cups of water to the bottom.

2. In a large mixing bowl, thoroughly combine ground turkey, pork, breadcrumbs, Romano cheese, Worcestershire sauce, egg, salt, black pepper, scallions, and garlic.

3. Shape this mixture into a meatloaf; place the meatloaf in a baking dish and lower the dish onto the rack.

4. Then, in a mixing bowl, thoroughly combine puréed tomatoes, ketchup, water, and Old Sub Sailor seasoning. Spread this mixture over the top of your meatloaf.

5. Secure the lid. Choose the "Meat/Stew" setting and cook for 20 minutes at High pressure. Once cooking is complete, use a natural pressure release; carefully remove the lid.

6. You can place the meatloaf under the preheated broiler for 4 to 6 minutes if desired. Let cool completely.

Storing

1. Wrap your meatloaf tightly with heavy-duty aluminum foil or plastic wrap. Then, keep in your refrigerator for up to 3 to 4 days.

2. For freezing, wrap your meatloaf tightly to prevent freezer burn. Freeze up to 3 to 4 months. Defrost in the refrigerator. Bon appétit!

47. Prize-Winning Chicken and Mushrooms

6 Servings

Ready in about
20 minutes

PER SERVING:
296 Calories; 19.6g Fat;
4.9g Carbs; 26.3g Protein;
0.2g Sugars

Make an authentic-tasting Thai chicken in the Instant Pot. Serve over hot
wild rice.

Ingredients

- 1 tablespoon peanut oil
- 1 ½ pounds chicken breast, cubed
- 1 stalk lemongrass
- 1/2 teaspoon cayenne pepper
- Salt and freshly ground black pepper, to taste
- 1 tablespoon red Thai curry paste

- 1 ½ cups button mushrooms, sliced
- 2 garlic cloves, minced
- 1 cup vegetable broth
- 1 tablespoon fish sauce
- 1 cup coconut cream
- 1 tablespoon fresh coriander

Directions

1. Press the "Sauté" button to heat up the Instant Pot; heat the oil. Once hot, cook the chicken for 5 minutes, stirring periodically.

2. Add the lemongrass, cayenne pepper, salt, black pepper, and Thai curry paste, mushrooms, and garlic. Continue to sauté for 3 minutes more or until the mushrooms are fragrant.

3. Now, stir in vegetable broth and fish sauce.

4. Secure the lid. Choose the "Manual" setting and cook for 10 minutes at High pressure. Once cooking is complete, use a quick pressure release; carefully remove the lid.

5. Afterwards, fold in the coconut cream; press the "Sauté" button and stir until the sauce is reduced and thickened. Garnish with fresh coriander. Let cool completely.

Storing

1. Place the chicken and mushrooms in airtight containers or Ziploc bags; keep in your refrigerator for 3 to 4 days.

2. For freezing, place them in airtight containers or heavy-duty freezer bags. It will maintain the best quality for about 4 months. Defrost in the refrigerator. Enjoy!

48. MEXICAN-STYLE CHICKEN CARNITAS

6 Servings

Ready in about 25 minutes

PER SERVING:
227 Calories; 9g Fat; 3.1g Carbs; 31.9g Protein; 1.7g Sugars

Here is a perfect chicken recipe for your weekend fiesta. The Instant Pot makes it faster than take-out.

Ingredients

- 2 pounds chicken stew meat, cut into pieces
- 2 cloves garlic, pressed
- 1 teaspoon chili powder
- 1 teaspoon dried Mexican oregano
- 2 tablespoons olive oil
- 2/3 cup vegetable stock
- Sea salt and ground black pepper, to taste
- 1/2 teaspoon paprika
- 1/3 cup apple juice
- 2 tablespoons fresh coriander, chopped

Directions

1. Simply throw all of the above ingredients, except for coriander, in the Instant Pot.

2. Secure the lid. Choose the "Poultry" setting and cook for 15 minutes. Once cooking is complete, use a quick pressure release; carefully remove the lid.

3. Shred the chicken with two forks. Spread chicken on a sheet pan and broil for 7 minutes until crispy.

4. Add fresh coriander leaves. Let cool completely.

Storing

1. Place chicken carnitas in airtight containers or Ziploc bags; keep in the refrigerator for 3 to 4 days.

2. For freezing, place chicken carnitas in airtight containers or heavy-duty freezer bags. It will maintain the best quality for about 4 months. Defrost in the refrigerator. Enjoy!

49. Prize-Winning Meatballs

6 Servings

Ready in about
15 minutes

PER SERVING:
476 Calories; 24.5g
Fat; 33.2g Carbs; 27.9g
Protein; 19.5g Sugars

Here is a great idea for your next fiesta party! Serve with hot
cooked rice or pasta.

Ingredients

- 1 pound ground pork
- 2 slices bacon, chopped
- 1 white onion, minced
- 1 teaspoon garlic, minced
- 1/3 cup tortilla chips, crushed
- 1/2 cup Romano cheese, freshly grated
- 1 egg

- Sea salt and ground black pepper, to taste
- 1 teaspoon dried marjoram
- 1 cup ketchup
- 2 cups tomato sauce
- 2 chipotle chile in adobo
- 2 tablespoons fresh cilantro

Directions

1. Thoroughly combine ground pork, bacon, onion, garlic, tortilla chips, Romano cheese, egg, salt, black pepper, and marjoram. Shape the mixture into balls.

2. Now, add ketchup, tomato sauce, and chipotle chile in adobo to the Instant Pot. Place the meatballs in your Instant Pot.

3. Secure the lid. Choose the "Manual" setting and cook at High pressure for 6 minutes. Once cooking is complete, use a quick pressure release; carefully remove the lid.

4. Garnish with fresh cilantro. Let cool completely.

Storing

1. Place the meatballs in airtight containers or Ziploc bags; keep in your refrigerator for up to 3 to 4 days.

2. Freeze the meatballs in airtight containers or heavy-duty freezer bags. Freeze up to 3 to 4 months. To defrost, slowly reheat in a saucepan. Bon appétit!

50. SAUCY PILAF WITH GROUND BEEF

4 Servings

Ready in about
15 minutes

PER SERVING:
493 Calories; 28.8g
Fat; 34.9g Carbs; 42.1g
Protein; 3.3g Sugars

Pilaf recipes seem complicated at first glance. The truth is that you do not have to spend hours in the kitchen to create this amazing one-pot meal. It takes only 15 minutes in the Instant Pot electric pressure cooker.

Ingredients

- 1 tablespoon sesame oil
- 1/2 cup leeks, chopped
- 1 teaspoon garlic, minced
- 1 jalapeño pepper, minced
- 1 (1-inch) piece ginger root, peeled and grated
- 1 ½ pounds ground chuck
- 1 cup tomato purée
- Sea salt, to taste
- 1/3 teaspoon ground black pepper, or more to taste
- 1 teaspoon red pepper flakes
- 2 cups Arborio rice
- 1 ½ cups roasted vegetable broth

Directions

1. Press the "Sauté" button to preheat your Instant Pot. Now, heat the sesame oil and sauté the leeks until tender.

2. Then, add the garlic, jalapeño and ginger; cook for 1 minute more or until aromatic.

3. Add the remaining ingredients; stir well to combine.

4. Secure the lid. Choose the "Manual" mode and High pressure; cook for 7 minutes. Once cooking is complete, use a quick pressure release; carefully remove the lid. Let cool completely.

Storing

1. Spoon your pilaf into airtight containers or Ziploc bags; keep in your refrigerator for up to 4 to 6 days.

2. For freezing, place your pilaf in airtight containers. Freeze up to 6 months. Defrost in the refrigerator. Bon appétit!

51. CLAMS WITH BACON AND WINE

5 Servings

Ready in about
10 minutes

PER SERVING:
157 Calories; 4.6g Fat;
27.7g Carbs; 3.4g Protein;
8.3g Sugars

Perfectly cooked clams with bacon and tarty white wine. Using the Instant Pot ensures even cooking, which is extremely important for a bright and flavorful seafood dishes. Serve alongside crusty bread and corn on the cob.

Ingredients

- 1/2 cup bacon, smoked and cubed
- 2 onions, chopped
- 3 garlic cloves, minced
- 1 sprig thyme
- 3 (6.5-ounce) cans clams, chopped
- 1/3 cup tarty white wine
- 1/3 cup water
- 1/2 cup clam juice
- A pinch of cayenne pepper
- 1 bay leaf

Directions

1. Press the "Sauté" button to preheat your Instant Pot. Add cubed bacon. Once your bacon releases its fat, add the onions, garlic, and thyme.

2. Cook for 3 minutes more or until the onion is transparent.

3. Add the clams, white wine, water, clam juice, cayenne pepper, and bay leaf. Secure the lid. Select "Manual" mode and cook at Low pressure for 4 minutes.

4. Once cooking is complete, use a natural release; remove the lid carefully. Let cool completely.

Storing

1. Place cooked clams in airtight containers or Ziploc bags; keep in your refrigerator for up 3 to 4 days.

2. To freeze, place cooked clams in heavy-duty freezer bags. Freeze up to 3 months. Defrost in your refrigerator. Enjoy!

52. SOUTH INDIAN CURRY

6 Servings

Ready in about
15 minutes

PER SERVING:
335 Calories; 19.9g Fat;
6.2g Carbs; 33.4g Protein;
2.9g Sugars

This is a traditional South Indian curry. Also known as Meen Kulambu, this dish can be made with any type of white fish.

Ingredients

- 1 tablespoon olive oil
- 1 cup scallions, chopped
- 1 teaspoon fresh garlic, smashed
- 2 pounds mackerel fillets, cut into bite-size chunks
- 1 ½ cups coconut milk
- 1 cup chicken bone broth, preferably homemade

- 2 dried red chilies, coarsely chopped
- 1 teaspoon curry powder
- 1 teaspoon ground coriander
- 1 teaspoon cayenne pepper
- Sea salt and ground black pepper, to taste
- 2 tablespoons freshly squeezed lemon juice

Directions

1. Press the "Sauté" button to preheat your Instant Pot. Heat the oil until sizzling; once hot, sauté the scallions and garlic until tender and fragrant.

2. Add the remaining ingredients, except for lemon juice, to the Instant Pot.

3. Secure the lid. Choose "Manual" mode and Low pressure; cook for 6 minutes. Once cooking is complete, use a quick pressure release; carefully remove the lid.

4. Drizzle with fresh lemon juice. Let cool completely.

Storing

1. Spoon Indian curry into airtight containers; it will last for 3 to 4 days in the refrigerator.

2. For freezing, place Indian curry in airtight containers or heavy-duty freezer bags. Freeze up to 4 to 6 months. Defrost in the microwave or refrigerator. Bon appétit!

53. Wax Beans with Parsley and Sunflower Seeds

6 Servings

Ready in about
10 minutes

PER SERVING:
115 Calories; 6.8g Fat;
11.2g Carbs; 4.2g Protein;
3.1g Sugars

Wax beans are made unbelievable tasty in no time thanks to the magic of pressure cooking.

Ingredients

- 2 pounds wax beans
- 1 red onion, finely chopped
- 1 teaspoon garlic, smashed
- 1 ½ cups chicken stock
- Black pepper, to taste

- 1/2 teaspoon cayenne pepper
- 2 tablespoons butter, melted
- 1 tablespoon fresh Italian parsley, roughly chopped
- 2 tablespoons toasted sunflower kernels

Directions

1. Add wax beans, onion, garlic, stock, black pepper, cayenne pepper, and butter to the Instant Pot.

2. Secure the lid and choose the "Steam" mode; cook for 3 minutes under High pressure. Once cooking is complete, use a quick release; carefully remove the lid.

3. Transfer cooked beans to a serving bowl; garnish with parsley and sunflower kernels and serve right now. Let cool completely.

Storing

1. Divide the mixture into six portions; divide the portions between four airtight containers; keep in your refrigerator for up 3 to 5 days.

2. For freezing, place the mixture in airtight containers. Freeze up to 10 to 12 months. Defrost in the refrigerator. Bon appétit!

54. CHEESE AND CREAM STUFFED PEPPERS

4 Servings

Ready in about
10 minutes

PER SERVING:
168 Calories; 8.8g Fat;
15.8g Carbs; 8.2g Protein;
8.2g Sugars

Your kids will love these mini peppers! They are so easy to make in an Instant Pot and they have a rich taste thanks to the spices and Cheddar cheese.

Ingredients

- 8 baby bell peppers, seeded and sliced lengthwise
- 1 tablespoon peanut oil
- 6 ounces Cheddar cheese, grated
- 2 ounces sour cream

- 2 garlic cloves, smashed
- 1/2 white onion, finely chopped
- Sea salt and ground black pepper, to taste
- 1/2 teaspoon paprika
- 1/2 teaspoon dill, fresh or dried

Directions

1. Start by adding 1 cup of water and a steamer basket to the Instant Pot.

2. Then, thoroughly combine all ingredients, except for peppers. Then, stuff the peppers with this mixture.

3. Arrange the peppers in the steamer basket.

4. Secure the lid. Choose the "Manual" mode and High pressure; cook for 5 minutes. Once cooking is complete, use a quick pressure release; carefully remove the lid.

5. Let cool completely.

Storing

1. Place stuffed peppers in airtight containers; keep in your refrigerator for 3 to 4 days.

2. Wrap each stuffed pepper tightly in several layers of plastic wrap and squeeze the air out. Place them in airtight containers; they can be frozen for up to 1 month.

3. To reheat, bake the thawed stuffed peppers at 200 degrees F until they are completely warm.

55. Zingy Portobellos in Sweet Sauce

4 Servings

Ready in about
10 minutes

PER SERVING:
89 Calories; 2.1g Fat;
14.2g Carbs; 6.2g Protein;
9.2g Sugars

The recipe works best with portobello mushrooms, but you can use any type of brown mushrooms you have on hand.

Ingredients

- 1 ½ pounds portobello mushrooms
- 1 cup vegetable stock
- 2 ripe tomatoes, chopped
- 2/3 teaspoon porcini powder
- Sea salt and ground black pepper, to taste
- 2 garlic cloves, minced

- 1/2 teaspoon mustard seeds
- 1 teaspoon celery seeds
- 1 tablespoon apple cider vinegar
- 1 tablespoon dark soy sauce
- 1 tablespoon brown sugar
- 1/2 teaspoon liquid smoke

Directions

1. Add all of the above ingredients to your Instant Pot; stir to combine well.

2. Secure the lid. Choose the "Manual" mode and High pressure; cook for 4 minutes. Once cooking is complete, use a natural pressure release; carefully remove the lid. Let cool completely.

Storing

1. Place your mushrooms along with sauce in airtight containers; keep in your refrigerator for 3 to 5 days.

2. Place your mushrooms in a plastic freezer bag for long-term storage and freeze them; they will maintain the best quality for 10 to 12 months.

56. MASHED CARROTS WITH CREAM AND CORIANDER

6 Servings

Ready in about
10 minutes

PER SERVING:
113 Calories; 6g Fat; 14.6g
Carbs; 1.5g Protein; 7.3g
Sugars

Make a quick and easy side dish that goes well with meatballs, grilled steak or fish fillets. A heavy cream adds dimension to the mashed carrots.

Ingredients

- 1 cup water
- 2 pounds carrots, chopped
- 2 tablespoons butter, room temperature
- 1 teaspoon paprika

- 1 teaspoon coriander
- Kosher salt, to taste
- 1/2 teaspoon ground black
- 1/4 cup heavy cream

Directions

1. Add water to the base of your Instant Pot.

2. Put the carrots into the steaming basket. Transfer the steaming basket to the Instant Pot.

3. Secure the lid and choose the "Manual" button, High pressure and 3 minutes. Once cooking is complete, use a natural release; remove the lid carefully.

4. Mash the carrots with a fork or potato masher. Add butter, paprika, coriander, salt, ground black, and heavy cream.

5. Taste and adjust the seasonings. Let cool completely.

Storing

1. Place mashed carrots in airtight containers or Ziploc bags; keep in your refrigerator for 3 to 5 days.

2. Place mashed carrots in freezable containers; it will maintain the best quality for 10 to 12 months. Defrost in the refrigerator or microwave. Bon appétit!

57. Chinese-Style Sticky Chicken

4 Servings

Ready in about
25 minutes

PER SERVING:
435 Calories; 12.3g Fat;
55.2g Carbs; 30g Protein;
41.9g Sugars

Take your chicken from blah to extraordinary by using the Instant Pot and the best ingredients!

Ingredients

- 1 pound chicken, cubed
- 1 teaspoon paprika
- Salt and black pepper, to taste
- 1/2 teaspoon cassia
- 1 tablespoon butter, melted
- 1/2 cup honey
- 4 garlic cloves, minced

- 1 ¼ cups water
- 1/2 cup Worcestershire sauce
- 1/2 pound mushrooms, sliced
- 1 teaspoon Sriracha
- 1 ½ tablespoons lemongrass
- 1 ½ tablespoons arrowroot powder
- 1/4 cup peanuts, chopped

Directions

1. Press the "Sauté" button to preheat your Instant Pot. Toss chicken cubes with paprika, salt, black pepper, and cassia.

2. Heat the butter and sauté the chicken for 4 minutes, stirring periodically. After that, stir in honey, garlic, water, Worcestershire sauce, mushrooms, Sriracha, and lemongrass; stir well to combine.

3. Secure the lid and choose the "Poultry" mode. Cook for 12 minutes. Afterwards, use a natural release and carefully remove the lid.

4. Press the "Sauté" button.

5. To make a thickener, add arrowroot powder to a small bowl; add a cup or so of the hot cooking liquid and whisk until they're combined.

6. Add the thickener to the Instant Pot and cook for 4 to 5 minutes more or until the sauce has thickened. Garnish with chopped peanuts. Let cool completely.

Storing

1. Place chicken in airtight containers or Ziploc bags; keep in your refrigerator for 3 to 4 days.

2. For freezing, place them in airtight containers or heavy-duty freezer bags. It will maintain the best quality for about 4 months. Defrost in the refrigerator. Enjoy!

58. TANGY PORK SHOULDER

6 Servings

Ready in about
55 minutes

PER SERVING:
511 Calories; 30.7g
Fat; 17.5g Carbs; 39.2g
Protein; 16.4g Sugars

This fancy pork dish might become your holiday favorite. With its specific mild flavor, Aji Panca chili will add just the right amount of excitement to your dish.

Ingredients

- 1 tablespoon lard
- 2 pounds pork shoulder
- 3/4 cup broth, preferably homemade
- 1/3 cup honey
- 2 tablespoons champagne vinegar

- 1 teaspoon garlic, minced
- 2 tablespoons soy sauce
- 1 teaspoon aji panca powder
- Kosher salt and ground black pepper, to your liking
- 1 tablespoon flaxseed, ground

Directions

1. Press the "Sauté" button, and melt the lard. Once hot, sear pork shoulder on all sides until just browned.

2. Add the broth, honey, vinegar, garlic, soy sauce, aji panca powder, salt, and pepper. Secure the lid. Select the "Manual" mode, High pressure and 50 minutes.

3. Once cooking is complete, use a natural release; remove the lid carefully. Set the pork shoulder aside keeping it warm.

4. Now, press the "Sauté" button again and add ground flaxseed to the cooking liquid. Let it simmer until the sauce has thickened.

5. Taste, adjust the seasoning and pour the sauce over the reserved pork shoulder. Let cool completely.

Storing

1. Place the pork in airtight containers or Ziploc bags; keep in your refrigerator for up to 3 to 4 days.

2. For freezing, place the pork in airtight containers or heavy-duty freezer bags. Freeze up to 2 to 3 months. Defrost in the refrigerator. Bon appétit!

59. Authentic French Cassoulet

6 Servings

Ready in about
35 minutes

PER SERVING:
376 Calories; 19.3g
Fat; 18.1g Carbs; 36.3g
Protein; 1.6g Sugars

If you are short on time, prepare this traditional cassoulet in your Instant pot for dinner! You can add a touch of hot paprika for extra flavor.

Ingredients

- 1 tablespoon olive oil
- 1 ½ pounds beef shoulder, cut into bite-sized chunks
- 1/2 pound beef chipolata sausages, sliced
- 1 onion, chopped
- 2 garlic cloves, minced
- 1 cup beef stock

- 1/2 cup tomato purée
- 1/2 tablespoon ancho chili powder
- Sea salt and ground black pepper, to taste
- 1 tablespoon fresh thyme leaves
- 1 (15-ounce) can white beans, drained and rinsed

Directions

1. Press the "Sauté" button and preheat the Instant Pot. Heat the oil and sear the meat and sausage until they are delicately browned; reserve.

2. Then, sauté the onion in pan drippings for 3 to 4 minutes.

3. Stir in garlic, stock, tomato purée, ancho chili powder, salt, black pepper, thyme leaves and beans.

4. Secure the lid. Choose the "Bean/Chili" mode and High pressure; cook for 25 minutes. Once cooking is complete, use a quick pressure release; carefully remove the lid. Let cool completely.

Storing

1. Slice your Cassoulet into six pieces. Divide the pieces between airtight containers; it will last for 3 to 4 days in the refrigerator.

2. For freezing, place each portion in a separate heavy-duty freezer bag. Freeze up to 2 to 3 months. Defrost in the microwave or refrigerator. Bon appétit!

60. Easy Fish Mélange

4 Servings

Ready in about
15 minutes

PER SERVING:
342 Calories; 20.8g
Fat; 14.7g Carbs; 24.6g
Protein; 9.2g Sugars

Try this all-star recipe for fish mélange with a Portuguese twist! This recipe is so simple to make in the Instant Pot and the balance of flavors is amazing.

Ingredients

- 1 pound fish, mixed pieces for fish soup, cut into bite-sized pieces
- 1 yellow onion, chopped
- 1 celery with leaves, chopped
- 2 carrots, chopped
- 2 cloves garlic, minced
- 1 green bell pepper, thinly sliced
- 2 tablespoons peanut oil

- 1 ½ cups seafood stock
- 1/3 cup dry vermouth
- 2 fresh tomatoes, puréed
- 1 tablespoon loosely packed saffron threads
- Sea salt and ground black pepper, to taste
- 1 teaspoon Piri Piri
- 2 bay leaves
- 1/4 cup fresh cilantro, roughly chopped

Directions

1. Simply throw all of the above ingredients, except for cilantro and lemon, into your Instant Pot.

2. Secure the lid and choose the "Manual" setting. Cook for 8 minutes at Low pressure. Once cooking is complete, use a quick release; carefully remove the lid.

3. Top with fresh cilantro. Let cool completely.

Storing

1. Spoon fish mélange into four airtight containers; it will last for 3 to 4 days in the refrigerator.

2. For freezing, place fish mélange in airtight containers or heavy-duty freezer bags. Freeze up to 4 to 6 months. Defrost in the microwave or refrigerator. Bon appétit!

VEGAN

61. Delicious Green Peas

6 Servings

Ready in about
25 minutes

PER SERVING:
173 Calories; 6.6g Fat;
22.7g Carbs; 7.7g Protein;
7.9g Sugars

This vegan dish literally cooks itself. In addition, it only takes about 25 minutes to make!

Ingredients

- 2 tablespoons canola oil
- 1 teaspoon cumin seeds
- 1 shallot, diced
- 2 cloves garlic, minced
- 2 carrots, chopped
- 2 parsnips, chopped
- 1 red bell pepper, seeded and chopped

- 2 bay leaves
- Sea salt and ground black pepper, to taste
- 1 teaspoon cayenne pepper
- 1/2 teaspoon dried dill
- 2 ½ cups green peas, whole
- 2 ripe Roma tomatoes, seeded and crushed
- 3 cups roasted vegetable stock

Directions

1. Press the "Sauté" button to preheat the Instant Pot. Once hot, add the oil. Then, sauté the cumin seeds for 30 seconds.

2. Add shallot, garlic, carrots, parsnip and pepper; continue to sauté for 3 to 4 minutes more or until vegetables are tender.

3. Now, stir in the remaining ingredients.

4. Secure the lid. Choose the "Manual" mode and cook for 18 minutes under High pressure. Once cooking is complete, use a natural release; carefully remove the lid. Let cool completely.

Storing

1. Spoon green peas into airtight containers; keep in your refrigerator for up to 3 to 5 days.

2. For freezing, place green peas in airtight containers or heavy-duty freezer bags. Freeze up to 10 months. Defrost in the microwave or refrigerator. Bon appétit!

62. Easy Traditional Barszcz

4 Servings

Ready in about
15 minutes

PER SERVING:
183 Calories; 7.3g Fat;
22.5g Carbs; 8.4g Protein;
7.7g Sugars

Bring some freshness to your everyday menu with this traditional soup that combines sweet red beets, vinegar, vegetables, and fresh dill.

Ingredients

- 1 ½ tablespoons olive oil
- 1/2 cup onions, chopped
- 2 garlic cloves, pressed
- Kosher salt and ground black pepper, to taste
- 1/2 pound potatoes, peeled and diced
- 2 carrots, chopped

- 1/2 pound beets, peeled and coarsely shredded
- 2 tablespoons red-wine vinegar
- 1 tomato, chopped
- 4 cups vegetable stock
- 1/2 teaspoon caraway seeds
- 1/4 cup fresh dill, roughly chopped

Directions

1. Press the "Sauté" button to preheat your Instant Pot. Heat the oil and cook the onions and garlic until tender and fragrant.

2. Add the remaining ingredients, except for fresh dill.

3. Secure the lid. Choose the "Manual" mode and cook for 10 minutes under High pressure. Once cooking is complete, use a natural release; carefully remove the lid.

4. Top with fresh dill. Let cool completely.

Storing

1. Spoon the soup into airtight containers or Ziploc bags; keep in your refrigerator for up to 3 to 4 days.

2. For freezing, place the soup in airtight containers. It will maintain the best quality for about 4 to 6 months. Defrost in the refrigerator. Bon appétit!

63. RICH RAINBOW CHILI

4 Servings

Ready in about
25 minutes

PER SERVING:
300 Calories; 11.4g Fat;
36.1g Carbs; 8.3g Protein;
7.9g Sugars

This is a complete family lunch that everyone will love. It requires only the Instate Pot so the clean up is minimal.

Ingredients

- 2 tablespoons sesame oil
- 1/2 cup red onion, sliced
- 2 cloves garlic crushed
- 1 roasted bell pepper, cut into strips
- 1 teaspoon habanero pepper, minced
- 1 pound sweet potatoes, peeled and cut into bite-sized chunks
- 1 cup vegetable broth
- 1 cup water
- Sea salt, to taste

- 1 teaspoon black peppercorns, crushed
- 1/4 teaspoon allspice
- 1/8 teaspoon ground clove
- 1 teaspoon sweet paprika
- 1/2 teaspoon smoked paprika
- 1 pound red kidney beans, soaked overnight and well-rinsed
- 1/2 (15-ounce) can tomatoes, diced
- 1/4 cup rum
- 1 (7-ounce) can salsa verde

Directions

1. Press the "Sauté" button to preheat your Instant Pot. Now, heat the oil; sauté the onion until tender and translucent or about 2 minutes.

2. Then, stir in the garlic and peppers; continue to sauté for a further 2 minutes. Now, add sweet potatoes, broth, water, spices, beans, and tomatoes.

3. Secure the lid. Choose the "Bean/Chili" mode and High pressure; cook for 15 minutes. Once cooking is complete, use a natural pressure release; carefully remove the lid.

4. Add rum and salsa verde. Press the "Sauté" button and continue to cook until everything is thoroughly heated. Let cool completely.

Storing

1. Spoon your chili into four airtight containers or Ziploc bags; keep in your refrigerator for up to 3 to 4 days.

2. For freezing, place your chili in airtight containers. It will maintain the best quality for about 4 to 6 months. Defrost in the refrigerator. Bon appétit!

64. Adzuki Bean Soup with Potatoes

4 Servings

Ready in about
30 minutes

PER SERVING:
474 Calories; 7.6g Fat;
84g Carbs; 20.5g Protein;
7.8g Sugars

Sriracha sauce is a Thai hot sauce made from chili peppers, garlic, distilled vinegar, sugar, and salt. Great alternatives for Sriracha include Louisiana hot sauces and harissa paste.

Ingredients

- 2 tablespoons olive oil
- 2 onions, chopped
- 2 carrots chopped
- 2 parsnips, chopped
- 1 celery with leaves, chopped
- 2 Yukon gold potatoes, peeled and diced
- 2 ripe tomatoes, pureed
- 12 ounces Adzuki brans, soaked overnight

- Kosher salt and ground black pepper, to taste
- 1 teaspoon cayenne pepper
- 1 teaspoon dried basil
- 1/2 teaspoon marjoram
- 1 teaspoon black garlic powder
- 1 teaspoon dried chive flakes
- A few drops Sriracha
- 4 cups boiling water

Directions

1. Press the "Sauté" button to heat up the Instant Pot. Now, heat the olive oil and sweat the onions until just tender.

2. Add the other ingredients; stir to combine well. Secure the lid and choose the "Manual" mode. Cook for 10 minutes at High Pressure.

3. Once cooking is complete, use a natural release for 15 minutes; remove the lid carefully.

4. Let cool completely.

Storing

1. Spoon the soup into airtight containers or Ziploc bags; keep in your refrigerator for up to 3 to 4 days.

2. For freezing, place the soup in airtight containers. It will maintain the best quality for about 4 to 6 months. Defrost in the refrigerator. Bon appétit!

65. BASIC VEGAN PILAF

2 Servings

Ready in about
15 minutes

PER SERVING:
291 Calories; 20g Fat;
35.4g Carbs; 11.3g
Protein; 2.8g Sugars

> Try this combo of garlic, onion, Arborio rice and spices. A festival in
> your mouth!

Ingredients

- 1 tablespoon olive oil
- 2 garlic cloves, minced
- 1 white onion, finely chopped
- 1 cup Arborio rice
- 1 cup water
- 1 cup vegetable stock
- 1/2 teaspoon dried basil
- 1/2 teaspoon dried oregano
- Sea salt and ground black pepper, to taste
- 1 teaspoon smoked paprika

Directions

1. Press the "Sauté" button to preheat your Instant Pot. Heat the oil and sauté the garlic and onion until tender and fragrant or about 3 minutes.

2. Add the remaining ingredients; stir to combine well.

3. Secure the lid. Choose the "Manual" mode and cook for 5 minutes under High pressure. Once cooking is complete, use a quick release; carefully remove the lid. Let cool completely.

Storing

1. Spoon your pilaf into airtight containers or Ziploc bags; keep in your refrigerator for up to 4 to 6 days.

2. For freezing, place your pilaf in airtight containers. Freeze up to 6 months. Defrost in the refrigerator. Bon appétit!

66. TASTY CABBAGE RICE

4 Servings

Ready in about
25 minutes

PER SERVING:
242 Calories; 13.3g Fat;
35.2g Carbs; 7.8g Protein;
10g Sugars

Purple cabbage, also known as red cabbage, is a powerhouse of precious nutrients. It boosts the immune system, promotes healthy bones, and fights chronic disease.

Ingredients

- 2 tablespoons olive oil
- 2 shallots, diced
- 1 garlic clove, minced
- 1 head purple cabbage, cut into wedges
- 2 ripe tomatoes, pureed
- 2 tablespoons tomato ketchup
- 1 cup basmati rice

- 1 ½ cups water
- 1 bay leaf
- 1/4 teaspoon marjoram
- 1/2 teaspoon cayenne pepper
- Salt and freshly ground black pepper, to taste
- 1/4 cup fresh chives, chopped

Directions

1. Press the "Sauté" button to preheat the Instant Pot. Heat olive oil and sauté the shallots until they are just tender.

2. Now, stir in minced garlic and cook until it is lightly browned and aromatic.

3. Stir in cabbage, tomatoes, ketchup, rice, water, bay leaf, marjoram, cayenne pepper, salt, and black pepper.

4. Secure the lid. Select the "Manual" mode and cook for 6 minutes under High pressure. Once cooking is complete, use a natural release for 15 minutes; remove the lid carefully.

5. Garnish with fresh chopped chives. Let cool completely.

Storing

1. Spoon cabbage rice into airtight containers or Ziploc bags; keep in your refrigerator for up to 4 to 6 days.

2. For freezing, place cabbage rice in airtight containers. Freeze up to 6 months. Defrost in the refrigerator. Bon appétit!

67. Colorful Lentil Stew

4 Servings

Ready in about
15 minutes

PER SERVING:
311 Calories; 22.9g Fat;
21.8g Carbs; 9.9g Protein;
6.7g Sugars

This delicious and nutritious lentil stew is easy to make in the Instant Pot. Black beluga lentils are protein-packed food with lots of health benefits

Ingredients

- 2 teaspoons toasted sesame oil
- 1 yellow onion, chopped
- 2 cloves garlic, pressed
- 1 teaspoon fresh ginger, grated
- 1 bell pepper, chopped
- 1 serrano pepper, chopped
- 1/2 teaspoon ground allspice
- 1/2 teaspoon ground cumin

- 1/2 teaspoon dried basil
- 1 teaspoon dried parsley flakes
- Sea salt and black pepper, to taste
- 1 ½ cups tomato purée
- 2 cups vegetable stock
- 1 cup beluga lentils
- 2 cups kale leaves, torn into pieces
- 1 teaspoon fresh lemon juice

Directions

1. Press the "Sauté" button to preheat your Instant Pot. Now, heat the oil; sauté the onion until tender and translucent.

2. Then, add the garlic, ginger, and peppers; continue to sauté until they have softened.

3. Add seasonings, tomato purée, stock and lentils.

4. Secure the lid. Choose the "Manual" mode and High pressure; cook for 8 minutes. Once cooking is complete, use a natural pressure release; carefully remove the lid.

5. Add kale and lemon juice; seal the lid again and let it sit until thoroughly warmed. Let cool completely.

Storing

1. Spoon lentil stew into airtight containers or Ziploc bags; keep in your refrigerator for up to 5 to 7 days.

2. For freezing, place lentil stew in airtight containers. Freeze up to 6 months. Defrost in the refrigerator. Bon appétit!

68. ZUCCHINI WITH SCALLIONS AND OLIVES

4 Servings

Ready in about
15 minutes

PER SERVING:
143 Calories; 9.4g Fat;
12.7g Carbs; 5.6g Protein;
4.4g Sugars

Zucchini is having a renaissance! They also cook wonderfully under
high pressure.

Ingredients

- 2 tablespoons garlic-infused olive oil
- 1 garlic clove, minced
- 1/2 cup scallions, chopped
- 1 pound zucchinis, sliced
- 1/2 cup tomato paste
- 1/2 cup vegetable broth

- Salt, to taste
- 1/2 teaspoon ground black pepper
- 1/2 teaspoon dried oregano
- 1/2 teaspoon dried basil
- 1 teaspoon paprika
- 1/2 cup Kalamata olives, pitted and sliced

Directions

1. Press the "Sauté" button to preheat the Instant Pot. Now, heat the oil; sauté the garlic and scallions for 2 minutes or until they are tender and fragrant.

2. Add zucchinis, tomato paste, broth, salt, black pepper, oregano, basil, and paprika.

3. Secure the lid. Choose the "Manual" mode and Low pressure; cook for 4 minutes. Once cooking is complete, use a quick pressure release; carefully remove the lid.

4. Add Kalamata olives. Let cool completely.

Storing

1. Spoon zucchini dish into airtight containers or Ziploc bags; keep in your refrigerator for up to 3 to 5 days.

2. For freezing, place zucchini dish in airtight containers. Freeze for 10 to 12 months. Defrost in the refrigerator. Bon appétit!

69. AUTHENTIC NEW ORLEANS GUMBO

4 Servings

Ready in about
15 minutes

PER SERVING:
196 Calories; 8.8g Fat;
22.7g Carbs; 9.6g Protein;
7.7g Sugars

This gumbo brings the flavors of New Orleans' cuisine into your kitchen! It is packed with nutrition and tastes so good.

Ingredients

- 2 tablespoons sesame oil
- 1 shallot, chopped
- 3 cloves garlic, minced
- 1 teaspoon jalapeño pepper, minced
- 1 celery stalk, chopped
- 1 carrot, chopped
- 1 parsnip, chopped
- 1/2 teaspoon dried basil
- 1 teaspoon dried parsley flakes

- 1 teaspoon red pepper flakes, crushed
- 1 1/3 cups lentils, regular
- 4 cups vegetable broth
- 1 ½ cups fresh or frozen chopped okra
- 2 ripe tomatoes, chopped
- Salt, to taste
- 1/2 teaspoon ground black pepper
- 1 teaspoon light brown sugar

Directions

1. Press the "Sauté" button to preheat the Instant Pot. Heat the oil; once hot, sauté the shallot until tender and fragrant.

2. After that, stir in garlic; cook an additional 30 seconds or until aromatic. Then, stir in the remaining ingredients.

3. Secure the lid. Choose the "Manual" mode and High pressure; cook for 12 minutes. Once cooking is complete, use a natural pressure release; carefully remove the lid.

4. Taste and adjust the seasonings. Let cool completely.

Storing

1. Spoon lentil gumbo into airtight containers or Ziploc bags; keep in your refrigerator for up to 5 to 7 days.

2. For freezing, place lentil gumbo in airtight containers. Freeze up to 6 months. Defrost in the refrigerator. Bon appétit!

70. Winter Mushroom Goulash

4 Servings

Ready in about
15 minutes

PER SERVING:
198 Calories; 9.1g Fat;
22.9g Carbs; 10.5g
Protein; 6.7g Sugars

Here's a protein-packed vegan dish that can be served for lunch or dinner. Cremini mushrooms contain about 3.1 grams of protein per 100 grams. Chickpeas contain 19 grams of protein per 100 grams.

Ingredients

- 2 tablespoons peanut oil
- 1 cup scallions, chopped
- 1 ½ pounds Cremini mushrooms, thinly sliced
- 2 garlic cloves, smashed
- 1/4 cup white wine
- Sea salt and freshly ground black pepper, to taste

- 1/2 teaspoon cayenne pepper
- 1/4 teaspoon dried dill weed
- 1/2 teaspoon dried rosemary
- 1 can chickpeas, drained well
- 1/4 cup fresh parsley, roughly chopped

Directions

1. Press the "Sauté" button and heat peanut oil. Now, cook scallions until they are tender.

2. Add the mushrooms and garlic; cook for 3 to 4 minutes, stirring periodically. Add a splash of white wine to deglaze the pot.

3. Season with salt, black pepper, cayenne pepper, dill, and rosemary.

4. Secure the lid. Choose the "Manual" mode and High pressure; cook for 10 minutes. Once cooking is complete, use a quick pressure release; carefully remove the lid.

5. Add chickpeas and parsley; stir to combine.

6. Let cool completely.

Storing

1. Place mushroom goulash in airtight containers; keep in your refrigerator for 3 to 5 days.

2. Place mushroom goulash in a plastic freezer bag and freeze for 10 to 12 months. Defrost in the refrigerator or microwave. Bon appétit!

71. PORRIDGE WITH PUMPKIN AND BERRIES

4 Servings

Ready in about
25 minutes

PER SERVING:
201 Calories; 1.1g Fat;
51.8g Carbs; 5g Protein;
31.9g Sugars

Learn to make a pumpkin purée from scratch. It is easier than you think. You can
make a big batch and freeze leftovers in containers or ice cube trays

Ingredients

- 2 ½ pounds pumpkin, cleaned and seeds removed
- 1/2 cup rolled oats
- 4 tablespoons honey
- 1/2 teaspoon ground cinnamon
- A pinch of salt
- A pinch of grated nutmeg
- 4 tablespoons dried berries
- 1 cup water

Directions

1. Add 1 ½ cups of water and a metal trivet to the Instant Pot. Now, place the pumpkin on the trivet.

2. Secure the lid. Choose the "Manual" mode and cook for 12 minutes under High pressure. Once cooking is complete, use a natural release; carefully remove the lid.

3. Then, purée the pumpkin in the food processor.

4. Wipe down the Instant Pot with a damp cloth. Add the remaining ingredients to the Instant Pot, including pumpkin purée.

5. Secure the lid. Choose the "Manual" mode and cook for 10 minutes under High pressure. Once cooking is complete, use a natural release; carefully remove the lid. Let cool completely.

Storing

1. Spoon the porridge into four airtight containers; keep in your refrigerator for up to 4 to 6 days.

2. For freezing, place the porridge in airtight containers or heavy-duty freezer bags. It will maintain the best quality for about 6 months. Defrost in the refrigerator. Enjoy!

72. SAUCY QUINOA WITH MUSHROOMS

4 Servings

Ready in about
15 minutes

PER SERVING:
401 Calories; 12.1g
Fat; 60.2g Carbs; 14.1g
Protein; 2.7g Sugars

Quinoa is a great source of protein; further, it also contains a significant amount of iron, magnesium and riboflavin. Quinoa is good for your skin, bones, and heart.

Ingredients

- 2 cups dry quinoa
- 3 cups water
- 2 tablespoons olive oil
- 1 onion, chopped
- 1 bell pepper, chopped
- 2 garlic cloves, chopped

- 2 cups Cremini mushrooms, thinly sliced
- 1/2 teaspoon sea salt
- 1/3 teaspoon ground black pepper, or more to taste
- 1 teaspoon cayenne pepper
- 1/2 teaspoon dried dill
- 1/4 teaspoon ground bay leaf

Directions

1. Add quinoa and water to your Instant Pot.

2. Secure the lid. Choose the "Manual" mode and cook for 1 minute under High pressure. Once cooking is complete, use a natural release; carefully remove the lid.

3. Drain quinoa and set it aside.

4. Press the "Sauté" button to preheat your Instant Pot. Once hot, heat the oil. Then, sauté the onion until tender and translucent.

5. Add bell pepper, garlic, and mushrooms and continue to sauté for 1 to 2 minutes more or until they are fragrant. Stir the remaining ingredients into your Instant Pot.

6. Add the reserved quinoa and stir to combine well. Let cool completely.

Storing

1. Spoon your quinoa into airtight containers or Ziploc bags; keep in your refrigerator for up to 3 to 5 days.

2. For freezing, place your quinoa in airtight containers. Freeze up to 1 month. Defrost in the refrigerator. Bon appétit!

Instant Pot Meal Prep | Vegan

73. BARLEY WITH BUTTERNUT SQUASH

4 Servings

Ready in about
45 minutes

PER SERVING:
360 Calories; 6.4g Fat; 70g
Carbs; 8.7g Protein; 2.2g
Sugars

These veggie barley bowls are sure to wow your family! Sprinkle with crunchy pepitas if desired.

Ingredients

- 2 tablespoons olive oil divided
- 2 cloves garlic, minced
- 1/2 cup scallions, chopped
- 2 cups butternut squash, peeled and cubed

- 1/2 teaspoon turmeric powder
- 2 cups barley, whole
- 4 ½ cups water
- Sea salt and ground black pepper, to taste

Directions

1. Press the "Sauté" button to preheat your Instant Pot. Once hot, heat the oil. Now, cook the garlic and scallions until tender.

2. Add the remaining ingredients and stir to combine.

3. Secure the lid. Choose the "Multigrain" mode and cook for 40 minutes under High pressure. Once cooking is complete, use a natural release; carefully remove the lid.

4. Let cool completely.

Storing

1. Spoon your barley into airtight containers or Ziploc bags; keep in the refrigerator for up to 3 to 5 days.

2. For freezing, place your barley in airtight containers. Freeze up to 1 month. Defrost in the refrigerator. Bon appétit!

74. Cauliflower Soup with Coconut Cream

5 Servings

Ready in about
25 minutes

PER SERVING:
176 Calories; 13.1g Fat;
9.3g Carbs; 7.9g Protein;
3.4g Sugars

This classic vegan soup consists of vegetables, coconut cream, and fresh herbs. It is creamy, nourishing and delicious.

Ingredients

- 1 tablespoon olive oil
- 1/2 cup white onions, chopped
- 1 teaspoon garlic, minced
- 2 carrots, chopped
- 1 parsnip, chopped
- 1 celery, chopped

- 1 head cauliflower, cut into small florets
- 1 zucchini, diced
- 5 cups vegetable stock
- Sea salt and ground black pepper, to taste
- 1/2 cup coconut cream
- 2 tablespoons fresh cilantro, chopped

Directions

1. Press the "Sauté" button to preheat your Instant Pot. Now, heat the oil until sizzling.

2. Sauté the onion and garlic until tender. Add the carrots, parsnip, celery, cauliflower, zucchini, stock, salt, and black pepper, and stir to combine.

3. Secure the lid. Choose the "Soup" mode and cook for 20 minutes under High pressure. Once cooking is complete, use a quick release; carefully remove the lid.

4. Add coconut cream and seal the lid; let it sit until heated through. Add fresh cilantro. Let cool completely.

Storing

1. Spoon the soup into airtight containers or Ziploc bags; keep in your refrigerator for up to 3 to 4 days.

2. For freezing, place the soup in airtight containers. It will maintain the best quality for about 4 to 6 months. Defrost in the refrigerator. Bon appétit!

75. Brussels Sprouts with Cilantro and Nuts

4 Servings

Ready in about
15 minutes

PER SERVING:
132 Calories; 5.7g Fat;
17.8g Carbs; 6.3g Protein;
5.9g Sugars

Brussels sprouts are so versatile. Bursting with flavor, this vegetable is great on its own or combined with nuts and other vegetables.

Ingredients

- 1 pound Brussels sprouts, cut into halves
- 1/2 cup water
- 1/2 cup tomato purée
- Salt and ground black pepper, to taste
- 1/2 teaspoon cayenne pepper or more to taste

- 2 tablespoons soy sauce
- 1 fresh lime juice
- 1/4 cup cashew nuts, chopped
- 1/4 cup fresh cilantro leaves, chopped

Directions

1. Add the Brussels sprouts, water, tomato purée, salt, black pepper, and cayenne pepper to the Instant Pot.

2. Secure the lid. Choose the "Manual" mode and cook for 4 minutes under High pressure. Once cooking is complete, use a quick release; carefully remove the lid.

3. Drizzle soy sauce and lime juice over the top. Add cashew nuts and fresh cilantro leaves. Let cool completely.

Storing

1. Place Brussels sprout in airtight containers or Ziploc bags; keep in your refrigerator for 3 to 5 days.

2. Place Brussels sprout in freezable containers; they can be frozen for up to 3 months. Defrost in the refrigerator or microwave. Enjoy!

FAST SNACKS & APPETIZERS

76. MUSTARD BARBECUED WINGS

3 Servings

Ready in about
20 minutes

PER SERVING:
204 Calories; 6.7g Fat;
23.1g Carbs; 13.2g
Protein; 20.1g Sugars

Are you craving barbecued wings? Try juicy, pressure-cooked chicken wings that are ready in 20 minutes.

Ingredients

- 1 cup water
- 6 chicken wings
- For the Barbecue Sauce:
- 1/3 cup water
- 1/3 cup ketchup
- 2 tablespoons brown sugar
- 2 tablespoons blackstrap molasses
- 1 tablespoon mustard

- 1 tablespoon cider vinegar
- 1 tablespoon olive oil
- 1 teaspoon garlic, minced
- 1 teaspoon chipotle powder
- 1/4 teaspoon sea salt
- 1/4 teaspoon freshly ground black pepper
- 1/4 teaspoon ground allspice

Directions

1. Pour 1 cup of water into the base of your Instant Pot.

2. Now, arrange the wings in the steaming basket. Transfer the steaming basket to the Instant Pot.

3. Secure the lid and choose the "Poultry" function; cook for 15 minutes at High pressure. Once cooking is complete, use a natural release; carefully remove the lid.

4. In a pan, combine all of the ingredients for the sauce and bring to a boil. Remove from heat and stir well. Add chicken wings. Let cool completely.

Storing

1. Place chicken wings in airtight containers or Ziploc bags; keep in your refrigerator for up 3 to 4 days.

2. For freezing, place chicken wings in airtight containers or heavy-duty freezer bags. Freeze up to 3 months.

3. Once thawed in the refrigerator, heat in the preheated oven at 375 degrees F for 20 to 25 minutes or until heated through. Enjoy!

77. Brussels Sprout Bites

4 Servings

Ready in about
10 minutes

PER SERVING:
145 Calories; 7.7g Fat;
15.5g Carbs; 7.3g Protein;
3.8g Sugars

Brussels sprouts are loaded with omega-3 fatty acids, vitamin C, vitamin K, vitamin B1, vitamin B6, manganese, copper, and dietary fiber.

Ingredients

- 2 tablespoons butter
- 1/2 cup shallots, chopped
- 1/4 cup dry white wine
- 1 ½ pounds Brussels sprouts, trimmed and halved
- 1 cup water
- Salt, to taste
- 1/4 teaspoon ground black pepper, or more to taste

Directions

1. Press the "Sauté" button to preheat your Instant Pot. Once hot, melt the butter and sauté the shallots until tender.

2. Add a splash of wine to deglaze the bottom of the Instant Pot. Add the remaining ingredients to the Instant Pot.

3. Secure the lid. Choose the "Manual" mode and High pressure; cook for 4 minutes. Once cooking is complete, use a quick pressure release; carefully remove the lid. Let cool completely.

Storing

1. Place Brussels sprout in airtight containers or Ziploc bags; keep in your refrigerator for 3 to 5 days.

2. Place Brussels sprout in freezable containers; they can be frozen for up to 3 months. Defrost in the refrigerator or microwave. Enjoy!

78. Spicy Deviled Eggs with Dill Pickle

6 Servings

Ready in about
15 minutes + chilling time

PER SERVING:
277 Calories; 21.9g Fat;
3.7g Carbs; 15.8g Protein;
1.4g Sugars

Update the classic deviled eggs with dill pickle and Sriracha. You can garnish these eggs with sweet Hungarian paprika if desired.

Ingredients

- 10 eggs
- 1/4 cup extra-virgin olive oil
- 2 tablespoons mayonnaise
- 1 teaspoon yellow mustard
- 1 tablespoon dill pickle juice

- 1/2 teaspoon Sriracha sauce
- Maldon salt and freshly ground black pepper, to taste
- 1 tablespoon fresh parsley, chopped
- 2 tablespoons dill pickle, chopped

Directions

1. Begin by adding 1 cup of water and steamer basket to your Instant Pot. Place the eggs in the steamer basket.

2. Secure the lid and choose the "Manual" function; cook for 5 minutes at High pressure. Once cooking is complete, use a natural release; carefully remove the lid.

3. Slice each egg in half lengthwise.

4. Transfer egg yolks to your food processor. Now, add the remaining ingredients; process until creamy and smooth.

5. Then, pipe the chilled filling mixture into egg whites, overstuffing each.

Storing

1. Place deviled eggs in an airtight container or Ziploc bag; transfer to your refrigerator; they should be consumed within 2 days.

2. For freezing, spoon out the yolk mixture from the deviled eggs. Add the egg yolk mixture to an airtight container or Ziploc bag.

3. Place the container in the freezer for up to 3 months. To defrost, let them sit overnight in the refrigerator until they are fully thawed out.

79. Sticky Baby Back Ribs

6 Servings

Ready in about
25 minutes

PER SERVING:
359 Calories; 17.9g Fat;
28g Carbs; 22.8g Protein;
25.1g Sugars

Baby back ribs with a sweet and sticky sauce that is enriched with whiskey and ketchup. This recipe is so delicious because pork ribs can take on different flavors.

Ingredients

- 1 ½ pounds baby back ribs
- 1 teaspoon salt
- 1/2 teaspoon ground black pepper
- 1 teaspoon smoked paprika
- 1/2 teaspoon ancho chili powder
- 1/2 teaspoon granulated garlic
- 1 teaspoon shallot powder
- 1/2 teaspoon mustard seeds

- 1 teaspoon celery seeds
- 1/2 cup whiskey
- 1 cup ketchup
- 1/3 cup dark brown sugar
- 1/4 cup rice vinegar
- 1 teaspoon fish sauce
- 1 teaspoon Worcestershire sauce

Directions

1. Season the ribs with salt, black pepper, paprika, chili powder, garlic, shallot powder, mustard seeds, and celery seeds.

2. Add the seasoned ribs to the Instant Pot.

3. In a mixing bowl, thoroughly combine whiskey, ketchup, sugar, vinegar, fish sauce, and Worcestershire sauce.

4. Then, pour the sauce into the Instant Pot.

5. Secure the lid and choose the "Meat/Stew" function; cook for 20 minutes at High pressure. Once cooking is complete, use a natural release; carefully remove the lid. Reserve the ribs.

6. Press the "Sauté" button to preheat your Instant Pot. Simmer the sauce until it has reduced to your desired thickness. Pour the glaze over the ribs. Let cool completely.

Storing

1. Place the cooked ribs in an airtight container; keep in your refrigerator for 3 to 5 days.

2. For freezing, place the ribs in airtight containers or heavy-duty freezer bags. Freeze up to 4 to 6 months. Defrost in the refrigerator. Reheat in your oven at 250 degrees F until heated through. Bon appétit!

80. ASIAN-STYLE COCKTAIL SAUSAGES

8 Servings

Ready in about
15 minutes

PER SERVING:
270 Calories; 20g Fat; 5.4g
Carbs; 16.4g Protein; 3.5g
Sugars

Cocktail sausages are a classic. We've just given them a new twist, adding Chinese seasonings, Dijon mustard, and ketchup.

Ingredients

- 2 teaspoons toasted sesame oil
- 10 hot dogs, chopped into thirds
- 1/2 cup ketchup
- 1/3 cup chicken stock
- 2 tablespoons tamari sauce
- 1 tablespoon rice vinegar

- 1 teaspoon chili powder
- Salt, to taste
- 1/2 teaspoon Szechuan pepper
- 1 teaspoon cayenne pepper
- 1 teaspoon Dijon mustard
- 1/2 teaspoon fresh ginger, peeled and grated

Directions

1. Add all of the above ingredients to the Instant Pot.

2. Secure the lid. Choose "Manual" mode and High pressure; cook for 5 minutes. Once cooking is complete, use a quick pressure release; carefully remove the lid.

3. Let cool completely.

Storing

1. Divide sausage into four portions. Place each portion in an airtight container; keep in your refrigerator for 3 to 4 days.

2. For freezing, wrap sausages tightly with heavy-duty aluminum foil or freezer wrap. Freeze up to 1 to 2 months. Defrost in the refrigerator.

81. MOM'S COCKTAIL MEATBALLS

8 Servings

Ready in about
15 minutes

PER SERVING:
319 Calories; 21.9g
Fat; 12.6g Carbs; 17.5g
Protein; 3g Sugars

Entertaining your guests and family during the holiday season doesn't have to leave you stuck in the kitchen all day long. Simply drop meatballs into the inner pot, press the button and enjoy!

Ingredients

- 2 shallots, peeled and finely chopped
- 2 garlic cloves, minced
- 1 parsnip, grated
- 2 carrots, grated
- 1 cup button mushrooms, chopped
- 1/2 cup all-purpose flour
- Sea salt and ground black pepper, to taste

- 2 pounds turkey, ground
- 2 tablespoons olive oil
- 3 ripe tomatoes, pureed
- 1 teaspoon dried oregano
- 2 sprigs rosemary, leaves picked
- 2 sprigs thyme, leaves picked
- 3/4 cup broth, preferably homemade

Directions

1. In a mixing bowl, combine the shallots, garlic, parsnip, carrots, mushrooms, flour, salt, pepper, and ground turkey.

2. Shape the mixture into small cocktail meatballs.

3. Press the "Sauté" button and heat the olive oil. Once hot, sear the meatballs on all sides until they are browned.

4. Thoroughly combine pureed tomatoes, oregano, rosemary, and thyme. Pour in tomato mixture and broth. Secure the lid.

5. Now, choose the "Manual" function; cook for 9 minutes at High pressure. Once cooking is complete, use a natural release; remove the lid carefully.

6. Let cool completely.

Storing

1. Place the meatballs in airtight containers or Ziploc bags; keep in your refrigerator for up to 3 to 4 days.

2. Freeze the meatballs in airtight containers or heavy-duty freezer bags. Freeze up to 3 to 4 months. To defrost, slowly reheat in a saucepan. Bon appétit!

82. SPICY PORK AND TOMATO DIP

10 Servings

Ready in about
20 minutes

PER SERVING:
226 Calories; 15.4g Fat;
2.2g Carbs; 18.6g Protein;
0.8g Sugars

With a high-quality ground meat, aromatic spices, and ripe tomatoes, this scrumptious dipping sauce is super addicting. Don't trust words and try it now!

Ingredients

- 2 tablespoons canola oil
- 1 pound ground pork
- 1/2 pound ground beef
- 1/2 cup leeks, finely chopped
- 1 garlic clove, minced
- 1 ½ teaspoons Cajun seasonings

- 1 teaspoon harissa spice blend
- 1/2 teaspoon cayenne pepper
- 1 teaspoon sea salt
- 1/2 teaspoon ground black pepper, to taste
- 2 ripe tomatoes, chopped

Directions

1. Press the "Sauté" button and heat the oil. Once hot, cook the ground meat, stirring with a Silicone spatula so that it gets broken up as it cooks.

2. Stir in the leeks and garlic; cook until they are tender and fragrant. Stir in Cajun seasonings, harissa spice blend, cayenne pepper, sea salt, and ground black pepper.

3. Add pureed tomatoes and secure the lid. Now, choose the "Manual" mode and cook for 13 minutes at High pressure.

4. Once cooking is complete, use a natural release; remove the lid carefully.

5. Let cool completely.

Storing

1. Place your dip in airtight containers or Ziploc bags; keep in your refrigerator for up to 3 to 4 days.

2. For freezing, place your dip in airtight containers or heavy-duty freezer bags. Freeze up to 2 to 3 months. Defrost in the refrigerator. Bon appétit!

83. STUFFED MUSHROOMS WITH CHEESE

4 Servings

Ready in about
10 minutes

PER SERVING:
304 Calories; 25.4g
Fat; 10.9g Carbs; 10.7g
Protein; 6.7g Sugars

Easy, cheesy and delicious, these stuffed mushrooms look spectacular on a serving platter. Consider preparing a double batch. Trust us!

Ingredients

- 2 tablespoons butter, at room temperature
- 1/2 cup scallions, chopped
- 2 cloves garlic, minced
- 1 cup cream cheese, at room temperature
- 1 cup cheddar cheese, grated
- 1 bell pepper, seeded and chopped

- 1 chili pepper, seeded and minced
- 1 teaspoon dried oregano
- 1 teaspoon dried parsley flakes
- 1 teaspoon dried rosemary
- 16 medium-sized button mushrooms, stems removed

Directions

1. Press the "Sauté" button to preheat your Instant Pot. Now, melt the butter and sauté the scallions until tender and fragrant.

2. Stir in the garlic; continue to sauté an additional 30 seconds or until fragrant. Add cheese, peppers, oregano, parsley, and rosemary.

3. After that, fill the mushroom caps with the pepper/cheese mixture.

4. Place 1 cup of water and a steamer basket in the Instant Pot. Arrange the stuffed mushrooms in the steamer basket.

5. Secure the lid. Choose the "Manual" mode and High pressure; cook for 5 minutes. Once cooking is complete, use a quick pressure release; carefully remove the lid.

6. Let cool completely.

Storing

1. Place stuffed mushrooms in airtight containers; keep in your refrigerator for 3 to 5 days.

2. Place stuffed mushrooms on the parchment-lined baking sheet, about 1-inch apart from each other; freezer for about 2 to 3 hours.

3. Remove frozen mushrooms to a plastic freezer bag for long-term storage; they will maintain the best quality for 10 to 12 months.

84. PARTY CHICKEN DRUMETTES

6 Servings

Ready in about
30 minutes

PER SERVING:
212 Calories; 10.7g Fat;
4.6g Carbs; 23.6g Protein;
3.2g Sugars

If you love spicy and tangy chicken, you'll go crazy for these chicken drumettes. This just might be the best way to use chicken for a party.

Ingredients

- 1 ½ pounds chicken drumettes
- Kosher salt, to taste
- 1/2 teaspoon mixed peppercorns, crushed
- 1/2 teaspoon cayenne pepper
- 1 teaspoon shallot powder
- 1 teaspoon garlic powder
- 1/2 stick butter, melted
- 2 tablespoons hot sauce
- 1 tablespoon fish sauce
- 1/3 cup ketchup

Directions

1. Prepare your Instant Pot by adding 1 cup of water and metal trivet to its bottom. Place chicken drumettes on the trivet.

2. Secure the lid. Choose the "Manual" mode and High pressure; cook for 6 minutes. Once cooking is complete, use a natural pressure release; carefully remove the lid.

3. Toss chicken drumettes with the remaining ingredients.

4. Arrange chicken wings, top side down, on a broiler pan. Place rack on top. Broil for 10 minutes; flip over and broil for 10 minutes more.

5. Top with remaining sauce. Let cool completely.

Storing

1. Place chicken drumettes in airtight containers or Ziploc bags; keep in your refrigerator for up 3 to 4 days.

2. For freezing, place chicken drumettes in airtight containers or heavy-duty freezer bags. Freeze up to 3 months.

3. Once thawed in the refrigerator, heat in the preheated oven at 375 degrees F for 20 to 25 minutes or until heated through. Enjoy!

85. PARMESAN CAULIFLOWER BALLS

6 Servings

Ready in about
25 minutes

PER SERVING:
194 Calories; 13.8g Fat;
6.5g Carbs; 11.6g Protein;
1.8g Sugars

Prepare these elegant cauliflower balls for the next potluck and delight your friends! They literally melt in your mouth!

Ingredients

- 1 pound cauliflower, broken into small florets
- 2 tablespoons butter
- 2 cloves garlic, minced
- 1/2 cup Parmesan cheese, grated

- 2 eggs, beaten
- 1 cup Swiss cheese, shredded
- 2 tablespoons fresh parsley, minced
- 1 teaspoon cayenne pepper
- Sea salt and ground black pepper, to taste

Directions

1. Prepare your Instant Pot by adding 1 cup of water and a steamer basket to its bottom.

2. Place the cauliflower florets in the steamer basket.

3. Secure the lid. Choose the "Steam" mode and High pressure; cook for 3 minutes. Once cooking is complete, use a quick pressure release; carefully remove the lid.

4. Transfer the cauliflower florets to your blender. Add the remaining ingredients; process until everything is well incorporated.

5. Roll the cauliflower mixture into bite-sized balls. Bake in the preheated oven at 400 degrees F for 16 minutes. Let cool completely.

Storing

1. Transfer the balls to the airtight containers and place in your refrigerator for up to 3 to 4 days.

2. For freezing, place the balls in freezer safe containers and freeze up to 1 month. Defrost in the microwave for a few minutes.

86. Two-Cheese Turkey Dip

10 Servings

Ready in about
15 minutes

PER SERVING:
253 Calories; 17.7g Fat;
4.2g Carbs; 19.3g Protein;
1.6g Sugars

You can bake this dip in a preheated oven at 350 degrees F about 20 minutes or until the top is golden brown. Otherwise, serve it directly from the Instant Pot.

Ingredients

- 1 tablespoon canola oil
- 1 pound ground turkey
- 1 onion, chopped
- 1 clove garlic, chopped
- 2 cups ripe tomato purée

- 1/4 cup vegetable broth
- 1 tablespoon Worcestershire sauce
- 10 ounces Ricotta cheese, crumbled
- 10 ounces Colby cheese, shredded

Directions

1. Press the "Sauté" button to preheat your Instant Pot. Once hot, heat the oil.

2. Then, cook ground turkey, onion and garlic for 2 to 3 minutes or until the meat is no longer pink. Add tomato purée, broth, and Worcestershire sauce.

3. Secure the lid. Choose the "Manual" mode and High pressure; cook for 5 minutes. Once cooking is complete, use a quick pressure release; carefully remove the lid.

4. Now, stir in cheese. Stir until everything is well incorporated. Let cool completely.

Storing

1. Place your dip in airtight containers or Ziploc bags; keep in your refrigerator for up to 3 to 4 days.

2. For freezing, place your dip in airtight containers or heavy-duty freezer bags. Freeze up to 2 to 3 months. Defrost in the refrigerator. Bon appétit!

87. The Best Little Smokies Ever

12 Servings

Ready in about
10 minutes

PER SERVING:
317 Calories; 21.5g
Fat; 12.8g Carbs; 17.1g
Protein; 8.2g Sugars

Little smoked sausages cooked in chili sauce and grape jelly. Yummy! How could you go wrong preparing lil smokies for a party?

Ingredients

- 2 pounds Little Smokies sausage
- 1 pound bacon slices
- 1 (12-ounce) bottle chili sauce
- 1 cup grape jelly

Directions

1. Wrap each sausage in a piece of bacon; secure with toothpicks; place in your Instant Pot.

2. Add chili sauce and grape jelly.

3. Secure the lid. Choose the "Manual" mode and High pressure; cook for 5 minutes. Once cooking is complete, use a quick pressure release; carefully remove the lid.

4. Let cool completely.

Storing

1. Divide sausage into four portions. Place each portion in an airtight container; keep in your refrigerator for 3 to 4 days.

2. For freezing, wrap sausages tightly with heavy-duty aluminum foil or freezer wrap. Freeze up to 1 to 2 months. Defrost in the refrigerator.

88. Barbecue Chicken Dip

12 Servings

Ready in about
10 minutes

PER SERVING:
179 Calories; 7.5g Fat;
14.3g Carbs; 12.9g
Protein; 10.3g Sugars

Here's your new go-to party appetizer! It is perfect for dipping crackers, chips, pretzel bun bites or veggie sticks in.

Ingredients

- 1 pound chicken white meat, boneless
- 1 cup barbecue sauce
- 1/3 cup water
- 6 ounces Ricotta cheese
- 3 ounces blue cheese dressing

- 1 parsnip, chopped
- 1/2 teaspoon dried rosemary
- 1/2 teaspoon cayenne pepper
- 1/4 teaspoon ground black pepper, or more to taste
- Sea salt, to taste

Directions

1. Place all of the above ingredients in your Instant Pot.

2. Secure the lid. Choose the "Manual" mode and High pressure; cook for 6 minutes. Once cooking is complete, use a natural pressure release; carefully remove the lid.

3. Let cool completely.

Storing

1. Place your dip in airtight containers or Ziploc bags; keep in your refrigerator for up to 3 to 4 days.

2. For freezing, place your dip in airtight containers or heavy-duty freezer bags. Freeze up to 2 to 3 months. Defrost in the refrigerator.

89. Chunky Sausage Dipping Sauce

12 Servings

Ready in about
20 minutes

PER SERVING:
157 Calories; 11.4g Fat;
6.3g Carbs; 8.1g Protein;
4.1g Sugars

If you love cream cheese and sausage, you will love this easy, creamy and spicy dip. It will be a hit for a party!

Ingredients

- 1 tablespoon canola oil
- 1 pound turkey smoked sausage
- 1 (28-ounce) can tomatoes, crushed
- 1/2 cup water
- 2 red chili peppers, minced
- 1 teaspoon yellow mustard

- 1 teaspoon basil
- 1 teaspoon oregano
- 1 (8-oz) package cream cheese, at room temperature
- 1/2 cup sour cream

Directions

1. Press the "Sauté" button to preheat your Instant Pot. Once hot, heat the oil. Then, cook the sausage until it is delicately browned, crumbling it with a fork.

2. Then, add canned tomatoes, water, peppers, mustard, basil, and oregano.

3. Secure the lid. Choose the "Manual" mode and cook for 6 minutes under High pressure. Once cooking is complete, use a natural release; carefully remove the lid.

4. Add cream cheese and sour cream; seal the lid. Allow it to sit for at least 5 minutes or until heated through. Let cool completely.

Storing

1. Place your dip in airtight containers or Ziploc bags; keep in your refrigerator for up to 3 to 4 days.

2. For freezing, place your dip in airtight containers or heavy-duty freezer bags. Freeze up to 2 to 3 months. Defrost in the refrigerator. Bon appétit!

90. BEST PARM MEATBALLS

8 Servings

Ready in about
15 minutes

PER SERVING:
241 Calories; 10.9g
Fat; 14.5g Carbs; 19.2g
Protein; 6.5g Sugars

If you use a lean ground chuck, you can add fat cheese and eggs. It all boils down to the balance.

Ingredients

- 1 pound ground chuck
- 1/2 pound ground pork
- 1 cup scallions, chopped
- 1/2 cup tortilla chips, crushed
- 2/3 cup Parmesan cheese, grated
- 1 egg, beaten
- 3 tablespoons full-fat milk

- 1 teaspoon garlic, minced
- Sea salt and ground black pepper, to taste
- 1 teaspoon dried oregano
- 1 teaspoon dried basil
- 2 cups tomato sauce
- 1/4 cup fresh mint, plus minced

Directions

1. In a mixing bowl, thoroughly combine ground meat, scallions, tortilla chips, Parmesan cheese, egg, milk, garlic, salt, black pepper, oregano, and basil.

2. Shape the mixture into balls using an ice cream scoop.

3. Spritz the bottom and sides of the Instant Pot with a nonstick cooking spray; add meatballs; pour in the sauce.

4. Secure the lid. Choose the "Manual" setting and cook for 9 minutes under High pressure. Once cooking is complete, use a quick pressure release; carefully remove the lid.

5. Sprinkle minced mint leaves over the meatballs. Let cool completely.

Storing

1. Place the meatballs in airtight containers or Ziploc bags; keep in your refrigerator for up to 3 to 4 days.

2. Freeze the meatballs in airtight containers or heavy-duty freezer bags. Freeze up to 3 to 4 months. To defrost, slowly reheat in a saucepan. Bon appétit!

DESSERTS

91. APPLESAUCE, CHOCOLATE AND PEANUT FUDGE

6 Servings

Ready in about
15 minutes

PER SERVING:
347 Calories; 22.3g Fat;
30.7g Carbs; 5.6g Protein;
21.4g Sugars

Here's a delicious way to end a party dinner! Make a fudge pudding in your Instant pot and see the difference.

Ingredients

- 8 ounces semisweet chocolate, chopped
- 2 ounces milk chocolate, chopped
- 1/3 cup applesauce
- 1 egg, beaten
- 1/2 teaspoon vanilla extract

- 1/2 teaspoon almond extract
- 1/4 teaspoon ground cinnamon
- 1/3 cup peanut butter
- A pinch of coarse salt
- 1/4 cup arrowroot powder

Directions

1. Add 1 ½ cups of water and a metal trivet to the Instant Pot. Press the "Sauté" button and add the chocolate to a heatproof bowl; melt the chocolate over the simmering water. Press the "Cancel" button.

2. In a mixing dish, thoroughly combine the applesauce, egg, and vanilla, almond extract, cinnamon, peanut butter and salt.

3. Then, add arrowroot powder and mix well to combine. Afterwards, fold in the melted chocolate; mix again.

4. Spritz six heat-safe ramekins with a nonstick cooking spray. Pour in the batter and cover with foil.

5. Secure the lid. Choose the "Manual" mode and High pressure; cook for 5 minutes. Once cooking is complete, use a quick pressure release; carefully remove the lid.

6. Let your dessert cool on a wire rack.

Storing

1. Cover chocolate fudge with foil or plastic wrap to prevent drying out. It will last for about 1 to 2 days at room temperature.

2. Cover with aluminum foil or plastic wrap and refrigerate for a week.

3. To freeze, wrap chocolate fudge tightly with foil or place in a heavy-duty freezer bag. Freeze for up to 4 to 6 months. Enjoy!

92. CHEESECAKE WITH BUTTER-RUM SAUCE

6 Servings

Ready in about
25 minutes

PER SERVING:
399 Calories; 23.7g Fat;
36.7g Carbs; 9.9g Protein;
34.6g Sugars

This silky and delicious cheesecake is so cute and so easy to prepare in the Instant Pot. For the best results, use any type of full-fat cream cheese like Philadelphia.

Ingredients

- 14 ounces full-fat cream cheese
- 3 eggs, whisked
- 1/2 teaspoon vanilla extract
- 1 teaspoon rum extract
- 1/2 cup agave syrup
- 1/4 teaspoon cardamom
- 1/4 teaspoon ground cinnamon

- Butter-Rum Sauce:
- 1/2 cup granulated sugar
- 1/2 stick butter
- 1/2 cup whipping cream
- 1 tablespoon dark rum
- 1/3 teaspoon nutmeg

Directions

1. Add cream cheese, eggs, vanilla, rum extract, agave syrup, cardamom, and cinnamon to your blender or food processor; blend until everything is well combined.

2. Transfer the batter to a baking pan; cover with a sheet of foil.

3. Add 1 ½ cups of water and a metal trivet to the Instant Pot. Lower the pan onto the trivet.

4. Secure the lid. Choose the "Soup" mode and High pressure; cook for 20 minutes. Once cooking is complete, use a natural pressure release; carefully remove the lid.

5. In a sauté pan, melt the sugar with butter over a moderate heat. Add whipping cream, rum, and nutmeg.

6. Drizzle warm sauce over cooled cheesecake. Let cool completely.

Storing

1. Refrigerate your cheesecake covered loosely with plastic wrap. Keep in your refrigerator for up to 7 days.

2. To freeze, wrap cheesecake tightly with foil or place in heavy-duty freezer bag; freeze for about 2 to 3 months. Bon appétit!

93. NUTTY CHERRY CRISP PIE

4 Servings

Ready in about
15 minutes

PER SERVING:
335 Calories; 13.4g Fat;
60.5g Carbs; 5.9g Protein;
38.1g Sugars

This cherry crisp is perfect for any occasion. You can use fresh or frozen cherries but make sure to use those that are sweet.

Ingredients

- 1 pound sweet cherries, pitted
- 1 teaspoon ground cinnamon
- 1/3 teaspoon ground cardamom
- 1 teaspoon pure vanilla extract
- 1/3 cup water
- 1/3 cup honey

- 1/2 stick butter, at room temperature
- 1 cup rolled oats
- 2 tablespoons all-purpose flour
- 1/4 cup almonds, slivered
- A pinch of salt
- A pinch of grated nutmeg

Directions

1. Arrange cherries on the bottom of the Instant Pot. Sprinkle cinnamon, cardamom, and vanilla over the top. Add water and honey.

2. In a separate mixing bowl, thoroughly combine the butter, oats, and flour. Spread topping mixture evenly over cherry mixture.

3. Secure the lid. Choose the "Manual" mode and High pressure; cook for 10 minutes. Once cooking is complete, use a natural pressure release; carefully remove the lid.

4. Let cool completely.

Storing

1. Place cherry crisp in four airtight containers; keep in your refrigerator for 4 to 5 days.

2. To freeze, place cherry crisp in four airtight containers or Ziploc bags; it can be frozen for 6 months. Defrost in your microwave for a few minutes. Bon appétit!

94. CHOCOLATE LOVER'S DREAM CAKE

4 Servings

Ready in about
15 minutes

PER SERVING:
299 Calories; 17.2g
Fat; 24.8g Carbs; 14.8g
Protein; 18.6g Sugars

A perfect dessert for any occasion, festive or not. Add cocoa powder, cream and nutmeg to get a classic mousse flavor.

Ingredients

- 1/2 cup granulated sugar
- 1/3 cup cocoa powder
- 2 tablespoons carob powder
- 2/3 cup whipping cream
- 1 cup coconut milk
- 1 teaspoon vanilla

- 1/2 teaspoon hazelnut extract
- 5 eggs, well-beaten
- 1/4 teaspoon nutmeg, preferably freshly grated
- A pinch of coarse salt

Directions

1. In a sauté pan, melt the sugar, cocoa powder, carob powder, cream, milk, vanilla, and hazelnut extract over medium-low heat; whisk until everything is well incorporated and melted.

2. Fold in the eggs; whisk to combine well. Add nutmeg and salt. Divide the mixture among jars.

3. Place 1 cup of water and a metal trivet in the Instant Pot.

4. Secure the lid. Choose the "Manual" and cook at High pressure for 7 minutes. Once cooking is complete, use a quick pressure release; carefully remove the lid.

5. Let cool completely.

Storing

1. Cover your cakes loosely with aluminum foil or plastic wrap and refrigerate for 3 to 4 days.

2. To freeze, place the cakes on a baking pan and freeze for 2 hours; then, place in a heavy-duty freezer bag. It will maintain the best quality for about 2 to 3 months. Enjoy!

95. FESTIVE UPSIDE-DOWN CAKE

8 Servings

Ready in about
45 minutes

PER SERVING:
354 Calories; 13.1g Fat;
55.4g Carbs; 4.3g Protein;
37.1g Sugars

This totally yummy cake is loaded with blood oranges, butter, and spices. It will definitely impress your guests.

Ingredients

- Nonstick cooking spray
- 3 teaspoons granulated sugar
- 3 blood oranges, peeled and cut into slices
- 1 egg plus 1 egg yolk, beaten
- 1 cup sugar
- 1 stick butter, at room temperature
- 1/3 cup plain 2% yogurt

- 1/2 teaspoon ground cloves
- 1/4 teaspoon ground cardamom
- 1/4 teaspoon ginger flavoring
- 2 tablespoons fresh orange juice
- 1 1/3 cups cake flour
- 1 ½ teaspoons baking powder
- A pinch of table salt

Directions

1. Spritz a baking pan with a nonstick cooking spray. Now, arrange the orange slices in the bottom your pan.

2. In a mixing bowl, whisk the eggs until they are frothy. Now, add the sugar and mix well. Stir in the butter and mix again.

3. After that, add yogurt, cloves, cardamom, ginger flavoring, and fresh orange juice. In another mixing bowl, thoroughly combine the flour with baking powder and salt.

4. Slowly and gradually, stir the flour mixture into the wet egg mixture; pour the batter on top of the orange slices.

5. Add 1 cup of water and a metal trivet to the bottom of your Instant Pot. Lower the baking pan onto the trivet.

6. Secure the lid. Choose the "Soup" mode and cook for 40 minutes at High pressure. Once cooking is complete, use a quick release; remove the lid carefully.

7. Place a platter on the cake and invert the baking pan, lifting it to reveal the oranges on top. Let cool completely.

Storing

1. Cover your cake loosely with aluminum foil or plastic wrap and refrigerate for 5 days.

2. To freeze, wrap your cake tightly with aluminum foil or plastic freezer wrap, or place in heavy-duty freezer bag; freeze for about 4 months. Enjoy!

96. The Ultimate Fudge Pie

8 Servings

Ready in about
10 minutes + chilling time

PER SERVING:
415 Calories; 36.3g Fat;
21.9g Carbs; 3.4g Protein;
20.8g Sugars

A giant pan of a sweet, gooey goodness! Cocoa butter, cream cheese, and coconut oil is a winning combination.

Ingredients

- 8 ounces cream cheese, at room temperature
- 4 ounces coconut cream, at room temperature
- 1/2 cup coconut oil
- 1/2 cup cocoa butter

- 1/2 cup peanut butter
- 1 teaspoon pure vanilla extract
- 1 teaspoon pure almond extract
- 2/3 cup almond flour
- 1/2 cup agave syrup

Directions

1. Press the "Sauté" button to preheat your Instant Pot. Add the cheese, sour cream, coconut oil, cocoa butter, and peanut butter to your Instant Pot.

2. Let it simmer until it is melted and warmed through.

3. Add vanilla, almond extract, almond flour, and agave syrup; continue to stir until everything is well combined.

4. Then, spoon the mixture into a cookie sheet lined with a piece of foil. Place in your refrigerator; refrigerate at least for 2 hours.

5. Cut into squares and freezer until solid.

Storing

1. Cover your fudge with foil or plastic wrap to prevent drying out. It will last for about 1 to 2 days at room temperature.

2. Place in airtight containers and refrigerate for a week.

3. To freeze, wrap your fudge tightly with foil or place in heavy-duty freezer bags. Freeze for up to 4 to 6 months. Bon appétit!

97. Vanilla Fruit Cake with Ice Cream

8 Servings

Ready in about
45 minutes

PER SERVING:
164 Calories; 0.3g Fat;
42.9g Carbs; 1.4g Protein;
16.9g Sugars

You no longer need to preheat an entire oven to bake a pudding cake – you just need an Instant Pot! Enjoy this easy and delicious ooey gooey pudding cake.

Ingredients

- Nonstick cooking spray
- 3/4 cup all-purpose flour
- 1/2 teaspoon baking soda
- 1 teaspoon baking powder
- A pinch of grated nutmeg
- A pinch of salt
- 1 stick butter, cold

- 1/4 cup vanilla cookies, crumbled
- 1/3 cup brown sugar
- 2 eggs, whisked
- 1/2 cup almond milk
- 2 cups blackberries
- 4 dollops of vanilla ice cream, to serve

Directions

1. Spritz a baking pan with a nonstick cooking spray.

2. In a mixing bowl, thoroughly combine the flour, baking soda, baking powder, nutmeg, and salt.

3. Cut in the butter using two knives; now, add crumbled cookies and sugar; mix until everything is combined well. Add the eggs and almond milk; fold in the blackberries.

4. Finally, scrape the mixture into the prepared baking pan. Cover with a sheet of foil; make sure that foil fits tightly around sides and under the bottom of your baking pan.

5. Add water and a metal trivet to the Instant Pot. Lower the baking pan onto the trivet and secure the lid.

6. Select the "Manual" mode. Bake for 30 minutes at High pressure.

7. Once cooking is complete, use a quick release; remove the lid carefully. Remove the baking pan from the Instant Pot using rack handles. Remove foil and allow the cake to cool approximately 10 minutes.

8. Let cool completely.

Storing

1. Cover your cake loosely with aluminum foil or plastic wrap and refrigerate for 6 days.

2. To freeze, wrap your cake tightly with aluminum foil or plastic freezer wrap, or place in heavy-duty freezer bag; freeze for about 6 months.

3. Freeze ice cream for 2 to 4 months. Enjoy!

98. SEMI-HOMEMADE CHERRY COBBLER

6 Servings

Ready in about
20 minutes

PER SERVING:
499 Calories; 16.2g Fat;
82g Carbs; 4.5g Protein;
24.3g Sugars

This cherry cobbler can be made quite easily in the Instant Pot. You can use a store-bought cake mix or make your own. It's up to you.

Ingredients

- 30 ounces cherry pie filling
- 1 box yellow cake mix
- 1/2 cup coconut butter, melted

- 1/2 teaspoon ground cinnamon
- 1/2 teaspoon ground cardamom
- 1/4 teaspoon grated nutmeg

Directions

1. Add 1 cup of water and metal rack to the Instant Pot. Place cherry pie filling in a pan.

2. Mix the remaining ingredients; spread the batter over the cherry pie filling evenly.

3. Secure the lid. Choose the "Manual" mode and cook for 10 minutes under High pressure. Once cooking is complete, use a natural pressure release; carefully remove the lid.

4. Let cool completely.

Storing

1. Place cherry cobbler in airtight containers; keep in your refrigerator for 4 to 5 days.

2. To freeze, place cherry cobbler in airtight containers or Ziploc bags; it can be frozen for 3 months. Defrost in your microwave for a few minutes. Bon appétit!

99. EASY ALMOND FUDGE BROWNIES

8 Servings

Ready in about
25 minutes

PER SERVING:
265 Calories; 16.4g Fat;
24.9g Carbs; 6.5g Protein;
12.4g Sugars

Conquer your next family gathering with this lavish dessert. Besides being super yummy, it is also easy to make in the Instant Pot.

Ingredients

- 3 ounces chocolate, chopped into small chunks
- 1/3 cup coconut oil
- 1/2 cup brown sugar
- 3 eggs, well beaten
- 1/2 teaspoon almond extract
- 1 teaspoon vanilla extract

- 2/3 cup all-purpose flour
- 1 teaspoon baking powder
- A pinch of salt
- 3 tablespoons cocoa powder
- 1 tablespoon carob powder
- 1/2 cup almonds, chopped

Directions

1. Microwave the chocolate and coconut oil for until melted.

2. In a bowl, thoroughly combine sugar, eggs, almond, vanilla extract, and melted chocolate mixture.

3. Add flour, baking powder, salt, cocoa powder, and carob powder; mix well to combine. Afterwards, fold in the almonds. Transfer the mixture to a lightly greased baking pan.

4. Add 1 cup of water and a metal rack to the Instant Pot. Lower the baking pan onto the rack.

5. Secure the lid. Choose the "Manual" mode and cook for 18 minutes under High pressure. Once cooking is complete, use a quick pressure release; carefully remove the lid.

6. Let cool completely.

Storing

1. Place your brownies in covered airtight containers to prevent drying out; keep in the refrigerator for 3 to 4 days.

2. For freezing, place your brownies in heavy-duty freezer bags and freeze up to 4 to 6 months. Defrost in your microwave for a couple of minutes. Enjoy!

100. Grandma's Pudding Cake

6 Servings

Ready in about
25 minutes

PER SERVING:
426 Calories; 26.4g Fat;
39.9g Carbs; 7.3g Protein;
17.3g Sugars

This old-fashioned pudding cake turns out great every time! What is the best part? Thanks to the Instant Pot, it will be ready in less than 25 minutes!

Ingredients

- Nonstick cooking spray
- 3 tablespoons crumbled butter cookies
- 1 stick butter, at room temperature
- 1 cup sugar
- 1/2 teaspoon pure vanilla extract
- 1/2 teaspoon pure coconut extract
- 3 eggs, beaten
- 1 ¼ cups cake flour
- 1/4 cup coconut milk

Directions

1. Spritz the bottom and sides of a steam bowl with a nonstick cooking spray. Add crumbled butter cookies to the bottom.

2. Then, beat the butter, sugar, vanilla, and coconut extract until very creamy; now, add the eggs, one at a time and continue to mix.

3. Stir in the flour and milk; mix to combine well. Scrape the batter into the prepared steam bowl.

4. Secure the lid. Choose the "Steam" mode and cook for 20 minutes under High pressure. Once cooking is complete, use a natural pressure release; carefully remove the lid. Let cool completely.

Storing

1. Cover your cake loosely with aluminum foil or plastic wrap and refrigerate for 7 days.

2. To freeze, wrap your cake tightly with aluminum foil or plastic freezer wrap, or place in heavy-duty freezer bag; freeze for about 4 to 6 months. Enjoy!

101. FUDGY GREEK YOGURT BROWNIES

6 Servings

Ready in about
25 minutes

PER SERVING:
270 Calories; 12.5g Fat;
41.1g Carbs; 6g Protein;
14.2g Sugars

It doesn't get more fudgy than these Instant Pot brownies! They have just become even better with an addition of eggs and Greek yogurt. Did you know that chocolate is a powerhouse of antioxidants?

Ingredients

- 1/2 stick butter, at room temperature
- 1 egg, beaten
- 2 tablespoons Greek yogurt
- 1/2 cup cake flour
- 1/2 teaspoon baking soda
- 1/4 cup cocoa powder

- 1/8 teaspoon salt
- 1/8 teaspoon nutmeg, freshly grated
- 1/2 teaspoon ground cinnamon
- 1 teaspoon vanilla extract
- 1/4 cup honey
- 1/4 cup chocolate, cut into chunks

Directions

1. Begin by adding 1 ½ cups of water and a metal trivet to the bottom of your Instant Pot.

2. Thoroughly combine the butter, egg, Greek yogurt, flour, baking soda, cocoa powder, salt, nutmeg, cinnamon, vanilla, and honey.

3. Fold in the chocolate chunks; stir to combine well.

4. Scrape the batter into a cake pan and cover with a piece of foil. Place the pan on top of the trivet.

5. Secure the lid. Choose "Porridge" mode and cook for 20 minutes under High pressure. Once cooking is complete, use a quick pressure release; carefully remove the lid. Let cool completely.

Storing

1. Place your brownies in covered airtight containers to prevent drying out; keep in the refrigerator for 3 to 4 days.

2. For freezing, place your brownies in heavy-duty freezer bags and freeze up to 4 to 6 months. Defrost in your microwave for a couple of minutes. Enjoy!

102. MINI CAKES WITH CHEESE FROSTING

6 Servings

Ready in about
35 minutes

PER SERVING:
320 Calories; 20.7g Fat;
29.6g Carbs; 5.9g Protein;
29.2g Sugars

Key lime brings amazing citrus flavor to these mini cakes. To serve, top with a grated lime peel. Enjoy!

Ingredients

Cakes:

- 3 eggs, beaten
- 3 tablespoons butter, melted
- 3 tablespoons coconut milk
- 1 teaspoon vanilla extract
- 1/2 cup coconut flour
- 1 teaspoon baking powder

- 1/2 cup agave syrup
- 1/4 cup fresh key lime juice

Frosting:

- 3 ounces cream cheese
- 3 tablespoons butter, softened
- 2 tablespoons agave syrup

Directions

1. Spritz the bottom and sides of four ramekins with a nonstick cooking spray.

2. In a mixing bowl, whisk the eggs with melted butter, coconut milk, vanilla, coconut flour, baking powder, agave syrup, and key lime juice.

3. Spoon the batter into greased ramekins and cover them loosely with foil.

4. Add 1 cup of water and a metal rack to the bottom of your Instant Pot. Now, lower the ramekins onto the rack.

5. Secure the lid. Choose the "Bean/Chili" mode and cook for 25 minutes under High pressure. Once cooking is complete, use a natural pressure release; carefully remove the lid.

6. Meanwhile, prepare the frosting by mixing cream cheese and butter with an electric mixer. Add agave syrup and continue mixing until everything is well incorporated.

7. Transfer the mixture to a plastic bag for piping the frosting on your cupcakes.

8. Let cool completely.

Storing

1. Refrigerate mini cakes covered loosely with plastic wrap. Keep in your refrigerator for up to 7 days.

2. To freeze, wrap mini cakes tightly with foil or place in heavy-duty freezer bag; freeze for about 2 to 3 months. Bon appétit!

103. Chocolate Almond Pot au Crème

3 Servings

Ready in about
15 minutes

PER SERVING:
304 Calories; 18.9g Fat;
23.8g Carbs; 10g Protein;
21.1g Sugars

This is a great base recipe for mini cakes so that you can make it with different spices and flavors.

Ingredients

- 3 eggs
- 2 tablespoons butter
- 3 tablespoons whole milk
- 3 tablespoons honey
- 1 teaspoon pure vanilla extract

- 1/4 teaspoon freshly grated nutmeg
- 1/4 teaspoon ground cardamom
- A pinch of salt
- 1 cup almond flour
- 3 chocolate cookies, chunks

Directions

1. In a mixing bowl, beat the eggs with butter. Now, add milk and continue mixing until well combined.

2. Add the remaining ingredients in the order listed above. Divide the batter among 3 ramekins.

3. Add 1 cup of water and a metal trivet to the Instant Pot. Cover ramekins with foil and lower them onto the trivet.

4. Secure the lid and select "Manual" mode. Cook at High pressure for 12 minutes. Once cooking is complete, use a quick release; carefully remove the lid.

5. Transfer the ramekins to a wire rack and allow them to cool completely. Let cool completely.

Storing

1. Cover your cakes loosely with aluminum foil or plastic wrap and refrigerate for 3 to 4 days.

2. To freeze, place the cakes on a baking pan and freeze for 2 hours; then, place in a heavy-duty freezer bag. It will maintain the best quality for about 2 to 3 months. Enjoy!

104. LIGHT AND ELEGANT ORANGE FLAN

4 Servings

Ready in about
25 minutes

PER SERVING:
343 Calories; 17.8g
Fat; 28.2g Carbs; 16.9g
Protein; 27.4g Sugars

There are so many recipes for a homemade flan out there, but you only need this old-fashioned recipe from a family cookbook.

Ingredients

- 2/3 cup muscovado sugar
- 3 tablespoons water
- 5 eggs, whisked
- 15 ounces condensed milk, sweetened
- 10 ounces evaporated milk
- 1/4 cup orange juice
- 1/2 teaspoon pure vanilla extract

Directions

1. Place sugar and water in a microwave-safe dish; microwave approximately 3 minutes.

2. Now, pour the caramel into four ramekins.

3. Then, whisk the eggs with milk, orange juice, and vanilla. Pour the egg mixture into ramekins.

4. Add 1 ½ cups of water and a metal rack to the Instant Pot. Now, lover your ramekins onto the rack.

5. Secure the lid. Choose the "Manual" and cook at High pressure for 9 minutes. Once cooking is complete, use a natural pressure release for 10 minutes; carefully remove the lid.

6. Allow it to cool about 4 hours.

Storing

1. Divide the mixture among four airtight containers; it can be stored in the refrigerator up to 3 days.

2. Slide the flan into pieces; transfer them to a heavy-duty freezer bag. Store in your freezer up to 1 month. Defrost in the refrigerator. Bon appétit!

105. DECADENT TROPICAL CAKE

8 Servings

Ready in about
30 minutes

PER SERVING:
258 Calories; 14.4g Fat;
33.2g Carbs; 1.8g Protein;
26.5g Sugars

Make this decadent fruit cake and delight your senses! Besides being incredibly moist and tasty, it turns great every time.

Ingredients

- 1 pound pineapple, sliced
- 1 tablespoon orange juice
- 1/2 cup cassava flour
- 1/2 cup almond flour
- 1 teaspoon baking powder
- 1/2 teaspoon baking soda

- 1/4 teaspoon salt
- 1/2 cup margarine, melted
- 1/2 cup honey
- 1/2 teaspoon vanilla extract
- 1/2 teaspoon coconut extract
- 1 tablespoon gelatin powder

Directions

1. Add 1 ½ cups of water and a metal rack to the Instant Pot. Cover the bottom of your cake pan with a parchment paper.

2. Then, spread pineapple slices evenly in the bottom of the cake pan; drizzle with orange juice.

3. In a mixing bowl, thoroughly combine the flour, baking powder, baking soda, and salt.

4. In another bowl, combine the margarine, honey, vanilla, and coconut extract; add gelatin powder and whisk until well mixed.

5. Add the honey mixture to the flour mixture; mix until you've formed a ball of dough. Flatten your dough; place on the pineapple layer.

6. Cover the pan with foil, creating a foil sling.

7. Secure the lid. Choose the "Bean/Chili" mode and cook for 25 minutes under High pressure. Once cooking is complete, use a natural pressure release; carefully remove the lid.

8. Lastly, turn the pan upside down and unmold it on a serving platter. Let cool completely.

Storing

1. Cover your cake loosely with aluminum foil or plastic wrap and refrigerate for 7 days.

2. To freeze, wrap your cake tightly with aluminum foil or plastic freezer wrap, or place in heavy-duty freezer bag; freeze for about 4 to 6 months. Enjoy!

Made in the USA
Lexington, KY
23 November 2018